Where Are The Miracles?

Rod O'Neil

ISBN: 978-1-60383-486-5

Published by:
Holy Fire Publishing

www.ChristianPublish.com

Printed in the United States of America and the United Kingdom

Book Dedication and Acknowledgements

This book is dedicated to my good friend, Jeff Carver, an avid bicyclist, marathon runner, triathlon competitor, church deacon, and radio station manager and broadcaster until a debilitating car accident left him unable to walk without assistance and trouble with talking effortlessly. His indomitable spirit to continue living for the Lord with severe physical handicaps and striving to regain some of his mobility has been an inspiration to all who know him. His openness to reveal his soul, his hurts, his challenges, his goals, and his hopes and dreams give insight to many scripture passages related to healings and miracles.

I also want to acknowledge my deep appreciation to my editor, Sue Ann Compton, for her thoughtful, professional, and insightful comments and edits. Sue Ann is a lecturer for the Department of English at the University of Louisville.

Acknowledgements also go to my publisher, Vanessa Hensel at Holy Fire Publishing and to my Publishing Specialist, Reta Haube, for going beyond the call of duty in helping me finalize the manuscript for printing. Their professionalism and dedication were heroic throughout the process.

FOREWORD

As pastor of a local church for more than four decades, rarely have I known a person like my friend, Rod O'Neil, who has the passion in accepting the challenge of pursuing a topic with as much commitment as *Where are the Miracles*?

This book is a product of Rod's long-time endeavor regarding the nature and continuance of healings and miracles performed by Jesus and His Apostles. Consequently, he has spent years of research and study, supported by personal experience, to arrive at his position on this topic, often discussed and debated by Christians with varying degrees of cessationist and continuationist viewpoints.

As Rod's pastor, I know the life of his faithful walk with our Lord Jesus Christ. I encourage you to read *Where are the Miracles*? with the goal of being informed, as well as inspired, to engage God's Word with the clarity and openness of mind to experience a significant insight for your own journey of faith.

Where are the Miracles? guides you to think with renewed interest about whether God works through healings and miracles in our present age as He did in the first century. You should read this book and reflect on its ideas as you consider how we can be faithful to the Gospel and our witness in today's ever-changing world.

Dr. Billy Compton, Senior Pastor
First Baptist Church
Mt. Washington, KY 40047

PREFACE

Then Gideon said "... if the LORD is with us, why then has all this happened to us? And where are all His miracles which our fathers told us about..." Judges 6:14

"Fools rush in where angels fear to tread" was penned by 18th-century English poet Alexander Pope. This quote somewhat adequately describes my quandary for writing this book. I firmly believe that our God actively intervenes in the affairs of men and that He is a God who wants to answer the prayers of His people. The quandary is that God is not working the wonders He once did during the time of Christ and the apostles. So what gives? Where are His miracles?

An atheist or a skeptic would be in the right to challenge us Christians for our claims of the miraculous, when in actuality, such claims are unverifiable, being coincidental, subjective, speculative, or even contrived or staged. No laws of nature seem to be broken by such miraculous claims.

From an atheist or skeptic perspective, it seems Christians are holding on to wishful thinking, and the best Christians can do is convince themselves that any fortuitous circumstances are a result of answered prayer from a god they have created in their own minds.

And to the chagrin of many faith healers, if we were able to invite and squeeze into one complex all of the big name faith healers we see on television and ask them to ply their abilities to heal any in a crowd of thousands who were sick, dying, infirmed, or crippled I have no doubt we would see many with "functional" or psychosomatic ailments rise up out of wheelchairs, and we would also hear claims from others that their pains or infirmities immediately lessened or even disappeared, but we would not see all healed, and we would not see any healed having true "organic" illnesses and infirmities. In other words, those having broken bones, missing teeth, mental retardation, Down Syndrome, burn victims, and amputees would leave without being healed, or even partially healed. I would venture to say not one faith healer can even heal a paper cut instantaneously, because God is not working supernatural healings and miracles today.

Those who claim healings from these Christian faith healers have the same type of functional ailments often cured by hypnotists, shamans, witch doctors, Satanists, and occultists. We have to ask ourselves some tough questions. Since nothing is too hard for God, and God can heal a headache as easily as He can raise the dead why, then, do we not see the hard "organic" cases being healed right along with the easier "functional" ailments? Could it be if God is not healing the hard cases He is also not healing the easier cases? Therefore, all the healings by so-called faith healers are not of God, but are, at best, of psychosomatic origin, and in the worst case, of satanic deception.

Where are God's unequivocal, objective, verifiable, and discernable supernatural healings and miracles today? Sure, some may say they heard of an arm growing back, or someone walking on water, or someone speaking and understanding an unlearned foreign language, or a dead man raising from the dead somewhere in the far reaches of Africa where the Gospel is just making an inroad – but even those cases do not stand up to the slightest scrutiny.

We can read in the four Gospels and Acts and see for ourselves that Jesus and His apostles healed anyone and everyone of anything and everything, anytime and every time, anywhere and everywhere they went, with no exceptions and with no one walking away only partially healed. If Jesus had not healed instantly and completely His critics would have easily said, "His healings were just a natural process, and He really hasn't done anything that hasn't already been done by others."

We can only surmise that the claims of supernatural healings and miracles we are seeing and hearing about today as compared to what Jesus and His disciples performed, are nothing but a sham. We need to take a hard and honest look at what Christians are calling healings and miracles of God and label them as something else, because they fall far short from being a true work of God as defined by Scripture.

God is a miracle-working God. That is part of His nature since He is by nature outside of nature. God even calls Himself Jehovah Rapha – the Lord that Heals (Exodus 15:26). By His sovereign design, God created the laws of physics and other natural laws to give us an ordered universe to live in and manage. Being omniscient, omnipotent, and sovereign, God can and easily does work within these established laws, else we would not be able to discern much of anything as being true if natural laws were continuously being broken. In fact, God is so sovereign, so omniscient, and so omnipotent, He can accomplish His will on earth without breaking the natural laws He has established for mankind.

Here is another one of my quandaries, conundrums, and even a twist of irony – those who claim to be working healings, miracles, and other wonders by the power of God and who call the rest of us faithless, heartless, and ignorant of the Scriptures and of the true power of God are actually the ones doing the most damage to the Church and to the reputation of the Holy Spirit. How? By deceptively, whether knowingly or unknowingly, attributing to God works of healings and miracles which are not of His doing.

These are some of the issues we will explore in this book. *Where are the Miracles?* is written for lay people within the Church by a lay person in the Church. I humbly submit this work to you, my peers – fellow laborers in the service of Jesus Christ. I hope you find this book thought-provoking, interesting, educational, and encouraging as you traverse through this world heading for the glorious future found only in Jesus Christ.

Contents

CHAPTER 1
INTRODUCTION

"...and you put to the test those who call themselves apostles, and they are not, and you found them to be false." Revelation 2:2

God, by his omnipotent, holy, and perfect nature still works miracles today, but there has been confusion in Christian churches since the end of the apostolic era what constitutes a miracle. This book addresses the most common types of miracles, which include supernatural miracles that seem to suspend or violate known laws of nature, providential miracles God works within His created laws of nature, and so-called demonic wonders which God allows Satan and his minions to work for the purpose of deceiving mankind – and if it were possible even God's very elect.

SUPERNATURAL VS. PROVIDENTIAL MIRACLES

This book also addresses how we discern whether or not God has suspended the workings of supernatural miracles and is only working providentially in the current church age. Those in the various Pentecostal movements (often labeled as the 1st Wave, 2nd Wave, and 3rd Wave) do not distinguish between marvelous natural wonders such as the birth of a child, or from supernatural miracles – those events that break, suspend, or violate a known natural law, or from those events where God seems to intervene in man's affairs through more natural or providential means. A miracle is a miracle is a miracle, so they say. Since Scripture, however, distinguishes between supernatural and providential workings of God, so should we.

Please note that throughout this book, all three waves of the modern Pentecostal or continuationist views are generally treated together using the broad term of Pentecostals.

Since the time of Christ the world has never seen a confirmed case of a broken bone being instantaneously healed, an amputated limb or even a severed finger miraculously restored, or of a single Down Syndrome individual having their genes corrected, and other mentally handicapped individuals having their IQ raised even by one point. These ailments would be classified in the medical field as "organic" disorders, where an organ is diseased, maimed, physically impaired, or even useless or missing. An organic disorder requires outside intervention to fix. A broken bone, for example, requires setting and several weeks to heal properly. Severe forms of cancer may require surgical and pharmaceutical intervention to remove or impede the growth of abnormal tissue and to restore the working order of the body.

Some forms of cancer, however, can easily fall into the "functional" disorder category. Functional disorders are those ailments where the normal body process is circumvented by a repair process. For example, a virus might cause a common cold which prompts the body to fight it for a few days. A relatively healthy body could recover from the symptoms of a cold and a fever in a few hours to a few weeks. Another functional disorder would include a paper cut on the finger. The body is marvelously designed to repair itself of many such ailments over time since we are *"fearfully and wonderfully made"* (Psalms 139:14).

Modern-day faith healers assert that church history is replete with healings and miracles, where people have been miraculously healed of all types of ailments since the times of the apostles – and they are correct. What they do not say, however, is the vast majority of those healings and miracles are tied to relic worship within the Catholic Church. Healings of various types, including unconfirmed stories of resurrections, have been received by praying to dead saints or touching relics such as a finger bone of a dead saint. The other miracles of the non-relic type are on the order of what has been found in cultic religions throughout the world – healings of functional disorders. A modern term would be psychosomatic healings.

Catholic Canonization. In April 2014, Pope Francis of the Catholic Church is expected to canonize two of his predecessors, John Paul II and John XXIII, as Saints. The Catholics have a very rigorous process they go through to acknowledge one of their own as an exemplary Saint within the heavenly kingdom. At least two miracles must be attributed to them. Canonization does not make a candidate a saint, but only acknowledges their sainthood based on attributable signs and wonders.

The Vatican group that reviews sainthood candidates is called the Congregation for the Causes of Saints. For each acclaimed miracle a team of doctors is assigned to first examine the miracle for its validity. Second, a team of theologians assess the miracle, and then they discuss amongst themselves the legitimacy of all the facts surrounding it. For the Vatican to certify a miracle, it must be instantaneous, permanent, and have no scientific explanation.

Affirmed Miracles by Pope John Paul II. Catholics attribute two miracles to the late John Paul II. The first miracle was the cure of a French nun, Sister Marie Simon-Pierre Normand, who was dying of Parkinson's disease. Her illness suddenly vanished when her order started praying on her behalf, and she wrote down Pope John Paul II's name on a piece of paper.[1] In 2011 the group claims the late pontiff also cured a 50-year-old Costa Rican woman. It is believed she was cured of a severe brain injury after her family prayed to the memory of the late pope and after a photo of John Paul appeared to talk to her. The miracle supposedly occurred in May 2011, the day of John Paul II's beatification, the first official step to being canonized as a saint.

Affirmed Miracles by Pope John XXIII. The Catholic Congregation of Rites has only confirmed a single miracle for the late Pope John XXIII. In May 1966 a nun, who doctors said was dying from internal ailments, quickly recovered after seeing a vision of the deceased pope. The nun said Pope John, who died two years before, appeared at her bedside and told her she would recover. The current pope, Pope Francis eased the Vatican rules by deciding that John did not need a second miracle to be canonized. Numerous other signs and wonders, though unconfirmed, have been attributed to John XXIII starting from the day of his beatification on 3 September 2000. These include about 20 reports of "graces and favors obtained

---

[1]http://www.christianpost.com/news/second-miracle-attributed-to-pope-john-paul-ii-set-for-fastest-sainthood-in-modern-history-98373/

from his intercession, [which has come in] from all over the world, often accompanied by medical documentation."[2]

Of course, Catholics look at these wonders as confirmation that God fully approves their belief system, to include all their teachings and traditions. The miracles confirm their doctrine, in other words. Catholics sincerely hope that non-Catholics would look at their confirmed signs and wonders and consider becoming a Catholic since God's hand is visibly seen on their church body.

Most Protestants, on the other hand, view Catholic miracles as spurious, coincidental, or psychosomatic in nature. Cessationist views within the Protestant camp would go one step further, and claim the miracles within the Catholic Church are on the same order as those claimed within the Pentecostal/Charismatic camp. Never has an organic healing ever been confirmed by Catholics or Pentecostals, and only those of a lesser origin, being quite subjective, are ever claimed.

No doubt, the healings attributed to John Paul II and John XXIII occurred. The questions remain, were they of God as the Catholics claim, or can they be attributed to other causes as non-Catholics claim? Being Protestant, our only recourse to determine the source of these healings comes from the Bible. Since the Bible never teaches we are to pray to any other powers other than to God, and the Bible does teach that for us to put our trust into other entities other than in God is idolatrous, we in the Protestant denominations come to a firm

[2]http://vaticaninsider.lastampa.it/en/the-vatican/detail/articolo/roncalli-papa-el-papa-pope-26469/

conclusion that the Catholic healings attributed to the deceased popes are not the workings of God.

Could Catholic healings be of Satan? It would be subjective and speculative, but it is not outside the realm of possibility. Consider this: just as easy as Satan can inflict diseases as he did with Job, Satan can also remove same diseases if it would further his aim to deceive the naïve and keep them from considering the truths found in the Bible. After all, it is easier to believe by sight than by faith.

Just as assuredly as God wants to bless His creation with good things, to include health and prosperity, Satan, on the other hand, wants to deceive people by using the same means – health and prosperity, the most sought after elements in our lives. We have to factor in such variables as we attempt to "prove all things" so we can discern what is true from what is false and misleading.

Christians have proven themselves to be a gullible and vulnerable lot. We tend to think no one is out to deceive us or take advantage of our generous nature since we have no compulsion to harm or deceive others. Therefore, many of us are very prone to scams, and we can easily be drawn after things which sound good, feel good, and have some kind of draw for us, such as a fix for any financial or health problem.

Also, since we often do not know with absolute certainty the validity of every situation, we have a tendency to go on blind faith and accept what we see and hear as being the gospel truth. Hence, all the more reason to depend on God's specific guidance found in His Word. This often includes questioning, investigating, assessing, validating, praying about, and discerning what comes before us.

But examine everything carefully; hold fast to that which is good;
1Thessalonians 5:21

A case in point, one of the more prominent deceptions recorded in the Bible involved Joshua and the Gibeonites. In brief, the Gibeonites, who were on the list to be annihilated as the Israelites marched into the Promised Land, opted to deceive the Israelites – and it worked. Posing as far-away travelers, they sought for terms of peace with the Israelites.

Joshua and his leaders asked some questions, but they did not investigate beyond these few questions and a simple visual inspection of the Gibeonites' shoddy appearance and old provisions. When the truth became known of the deception, Joshua and Israel were held responsible for the welfare of the Gibeonites all their days.

The men of Israel sampled [the Gibeonites'] provisions but did not inquire of the LORD. Joshua 9:14 [NIV]

If Joshua had asked God how to proceed with the Gibeonites, God could have revealed the truth to Joshua in some way, or God could have conveyed to him to investigate and validate the Gibeonites' story with a little bit more thoroughness. Israel could have been spared years of additional problems and wars from their close association with the Gibeonites.

Satanic deception was not an issue with Joshua and the Gibeonites. It was purely deception at the human level. The 18th century German author, Johann G. Seume, once said, "Nothing is more common on earth than to deceive and be deceived." How much more easily can we be deceived by Satan and his minions who use cloaks of righteousness and even clever healings and miracles to blind us to the truth?

Jesus actually commands us in Scripture not to be deceived by Satan, or be deceived by other men, or even be self-deceived. This means, we have some homework to do to guard ourselves from false teachings and even from false healings and miracles, which might closely mimic what we see in Scripture.

The miracles Jesus and His apostles and disciples performed were far above any work Satan can perform. God's creative miracles differ substantially from Satan's lying wonders. Benjamin Breckinridge Warfield, in his book *Counterfeit Miracles,* first published in 1918, presented several cases of "withered hands" being healed by several means: 1) by Faith Healers; 2) by Roman Catholic priests; 3) by mesmerism/hypnotism; 4) by one's own imagination (i.e., positive thinking); and 5) by deception.

We have to acknowledge not much has changed since the time of the apostles. By comparison, Warfield also said something remarkable about the miracles of Jesus: "The number of the miracles which [Jesus] wrought may easily be underrated. It has been said that in effect He banished disease and death from Palestine for the three years of His ministry."[3]

Crowds. This book takes a unique approach by showing how we can use Scripture to discern whether a proclaimed healing or miracle is truly of God or if it is of self, or possibly even of satanic origin. This approach begins not with the individual healings and miracles performed by Christ and His apostles, but of the Lord's dealings with crowds – large crowds. For example, in the Gospel of Matthew we find ten crowd situations where everyone is healed of any and every ailment.

As one looks at these dealings with the crowds several key attributes quickly come to the surface. These attributes include Christ and His apostles healing everyone of any and every type of disease, illness, and frailty from a fever to being dead and entombed for up to four days. There were no failures and no partial healings.

But by the time we get to the epistles, which were chronologically written after the incidences in the book of Acts, something drastically changed. In the epistles we see supernatural healings and miracles – the so-called "signs of an Apostle," presented in past (aorist) or perfect tense, or they were only worked by an authorized agent such as an Apostle or one that the Apostle's had directly anointed.

To help discern the truth of which miracles are truly of God and which are not, we need to mimic the Bereans who

[3]Warfield, B. B. (Originally Published 1918, Republished 2012). *Counterfeit Miracles.* New York: Charles Scribner's Sons (1918) and Forgotten Books (2012), 3

were depicted as being "more noble" because they searched the Scriptures daily to ascertain the truth of the Apostle Paul's words and actions (Acts 17:10-11). They did not search their own experiences or the experiences of others, but solely searched the scriptures, which were considered to be all-sufficient for determining God's truth, even back in the first century.

To assess the truthfulness of our doctrinal stances, one of the first things we should do is consider any and all assumptions and biases we might have. Our assumptions and biases define our perspectives on issues. In fact, many of our doctrines are built more on logical assumptions than on explicit biblical data. For example, we logically assume demons are fallen angels, but we have no explicit passage which clearly states such is the case. Even the doctrine of the Trinity is based on logical assumptions and implied teachings instead of explicit teachings from Scripture.

But first things first – what authoritative source(s) do we have at our disposal to give us the sound doctrines we crave and which enables us to determine God's truth? Is it the Word of God? Is it our own experiences? Is it someone else's experiences? Is it church tradition? Is it a combination of some or all of the above?

Most fundamental evangelicals hold to the concept of "*sola Scriptura*" – Scripture alone. If the Bible and the Bible alone is not our sole authoritative source for spiritual truth, then we have no way to prove what is dogmatically true. If we rely on "church tradition," which church do we use? If we rely on someone's experiences, whose experiences are reliable and authoritative, and how can we tell? If we rely on our own experiences, then what makes our experiences authoritative on the same level or even exceeding the authority of God's word?

We, therefore, first need to gravitate to the concept that the Bible is fully sufficient for determining the truth God wants us to have on this issue. Extra-biblical sources, and even experiences, are nice to have at times, but they are not required for determining the truth we are looking for in regards to whether or not supernatural miracles are being worked by God following the post-apostolic era.

Next, we need not only to identify our assumptions and biases, but we also need to question them for accuracy. We should never be afraid of challenging each other's perspectives, including our own. That is how "iron sharpens iron" (Proverbs 27:17) and how we find safety and victory in a "multitude of counselors" (Proverbs 11:14). If our assumptions and biases are incorrect, then our doctrines, which are based on them, could be incorrect as well.

There are smart theologians with doctorate degrees on both sides of the continuationist and cessationist camp. Whose position do we accept as correct? We all have the same Bible to read and study, so why are there so many different positions on biblical topics? The answer is because we all view biblical topics with differing assumptions and biases, which form our perspective or world view of interpretation.

Can those of us without seminary credentials and degrees discern sound doctrine? Yes, assuming our assumptions and biases are correct or correctable. Our assumptions and biases have to be challenged and corrected early on in our studies of any bible doctrine. More often than not, assumptions and biases are the old wineskins (Matthew 9:17), or the strongholds and fortresses which have to be demolished and rebuilt before someone converts from false doctrine to sound doctrine.

✦

"For the weapons of our warfare are not of the flesh, but divinely powerful for the destruction of fortresses." 2Corinthians 10:4

✦

We even have to come to terms with the terminologies we use in these debates on the supernatural. Here are some common definitions of the terms we will be using in this book.

DEFINITIONS

Cessationist: A view that God has suspended supernatural healings and miracles during this present age

Continuationist: A view that God still works supernatural healings and miracles during this present age

Gifts: Something received at a specific moment in time (e.g., moment of salvation, anointing or re-filling) which is fully developed and ready for immediate use at the discretion of the recipient (e.g. tongues, prophecies, etc.)

Miracles:

Supernatural: A spontaneous event which breaks known natural laws (e.g., walking on water, turning water into wine, creating and restoring a missing body part, raising the dead after burial or embalming)

Providential/Subjective: God works within His created natural laws to maneuver people, events, and circumstances to answer prayers and accomplish His will while maintaining an orderly world and not forcing skeptics to believe (e.g., finding a job or a spouse; healing through time and medicine, or changing the weather)

Spiritual: The ability of God to save and change a Hell-bound sinner into a Heaven-bound saint, and make them "new creatures" with new desires. No natural laws are broken in this process. Another type of spiritual miracle is demonic release. Again, no natural laws are violated

Demonic/Satanic: Deceptive wonders God allows Satan and his demons to perform

Pentecostal Waves

1st Wave. Early 1900s, following the Azusa Street revival, which helped propel Pentecostalism into mainstream

2nd Wave. 1960s, Charismatic intrusion into other mainstream denominations

3rd Wave. 1980s, Often called the Vineyard or the Word of Faith movement proclaiming a "Prosperity Gospel" and that signs, wonders, and miracles still exist today, with strong emphasis on healings and materialistic prosperity

DEFINITIONS

4th Wave. 2000s. More flamboyant behavior as noted by holy laughter in the Toronto Blessing and Brownsville revival movements. This movement is still ill-defined

Powers: Source of event or authority (e.g., God or Satan)

Prophecy: The foretelling of events or forth telling of the Gospel, depending on context

Psychosomatic Healing: A person's own mental state affects his health (e.g., someone in a wheel-chair walks when a 'mental block' is removed through trickery or persuasion; or a cancer patient is healed when his disposition changes from despairing to hopeful)

Signs: A term which groups miracles, healings, tongues, prophesies, and other phenomena to point to a specific purpose, person, or prophetic event

Talents: A skill or capability which is developed over time

Tongues: Ability to speak or hear in a language unlearned by the speaker/hearer (whether biblical tongues are known human languages, angelic languages, or unintelligible gibberish is still debatable)

Wonders: Attention grabbers, often used with signs (e.g., feeding of the five thousand)

Word of Knowledge and Wisdom: Definition and distinction are uncertain and still debatable even among continuationists

When studying the supernatural in the Bible, we see three possibilities for supernatural events:

1. Perhaps God used a known natural law, principle, or material to accomplish an unusual result. For example, God used wind to drive back the water of the Red Sea.
2. Perhaps God used a law of nature which has been suspended or has not yet been discovered or is simply beyond human understanding. For example, man once was able to live nearly one thousand years.
3. Perhaps what happened cannot be described by any natural law because God chose to suspend or violate a natural law. For example, someone walking on water.

We know what the Bible says, but what does it mean? One of the first rules of biblical hermeneutics, which involves the principles for determining an accurate interpretation, is "a text without a context is a pretext for a proof text." In other words, since the Bible can be used to develop any conceivable doctrine imaginable from Limbo to space aliens (because of our sometimes erroneous assumptions and biases), we must consider the context, the culture, the grammatical structure, the type of prose, and the whole counsel of God to determine the author's intended meaning and possible applications.

For example, Mark 16:16 says "*He who has believed and has been baptized shall be saved…*" Does this mean one needs to be baptized to be saved? Some Christians will say yes, others say no. Another example is found in Luke 10:19, "*Behold, I give unto you power to tread on serpents and scorpions, and over all the power of the enemy: and nothing shall by any means hurt you.*" Since most of the apostles died a martyr's death, do we have a contradiction in scripture or are there other extenuating circumstances we need to factor in? Other examples include the following:

- John 10:10 "*...I came that they may have life, and have it abundantly.*" Prosperity preachers take this passage to mean possessing an abundance of earthly things, while cessationists view this passage as believers having a purposeful existence while on this earth and for all eternity.
- John 14:12 "*...he who believes in Me, the works that I do, he will do also; and greater works than these he will do.*" Continuationists see this passage as strongly alluding to the continuation of the supernatural miracles Jesus worked, yet they would also admit no one can be found to have worked greater works than Jesus.
- 1Corinthians 15:29 "*Otherwise, what will those do who are baptized for the dead?*" There are over sixty interpretations for this passage. Mormons use this passage to justify their ritual of baptizing believers on behalf of dead unbelievers.
- 1Timothy 2:15 "*But women will be saved through childbearing...*" Most would agree this passage should not be taken literally, but metaphorically, to reflect that when men and women operate within their God-given design parameters, we are able to work at our peak performance, produce the spiritual fruit God wants us to have, produce less turmoil in our lives, and be better positioned to withstand Satan's deceptive ways.

Misuse of scripture within scripture. Any time Satan or an opponent of Jesus quoted Scripture it was never misquoted. It was either misapplied or they failed to consider proper hermeneutics. For example, in Genesis 3:1, the serpent [Satan] said to the woman, "*Indeed, has God said, 'You shall not eat from any tree of the garden'?*" Satan accurately quoted the essence of what God told Adam, but he said it in such a way as to raise doubt within Eve's mind. If you think about it, the biggest battle we fight has been the same battle fought since the days of Adam and Eve – the battle for truth.

In another passage, Mark 4:6-7, Satan said to Jesus, "*If You are the Son of God, throw Yourself down; for it is written, 'he will command his angels concerning you'; and 'on their hands they will bear you up, so that you will not strike your foot against a stone.'*" And Jesus said to him, "*On the other hand, it is written, 'you shall not put the lord your god to the test.'*" Again, Satan accurately quoted Scripture, but here he misapplied it to see if Jesus would fall into his trap.

Further in the Gospel of Mark, Jesus attempts to show the Sadducees the error of their doctrine for not believing in bodily resurrections because they failed to consider proper grammatical tenses within God's infallible word. Mark 12:26-27 reads, "*But regarding the fact that the dead rise again, have you* [Sadducees] *not read in the book of Moses, in the passage about the burning bush, how God spoke to him, saying, **'I AM*** [present tense] *the God of Abraham, and the God of Isaac, and the God of Jacob'? He is not the God of the dead, but of the living; you are greatly mistaken.*"

So, how should we biblically respond to someone who seemingly works a miracle, which seems to prove his doctrine? Virtually all religions claim healings and miracles. Can all such claims be truly of God? Catholics, Pentecostals, Muslims, Mormons, Buddhists, Hindus, Spiritists, Christian Scientists, mystics, hypnotists, Satanists, witch doctors, shamans, and even atheists claim to work miracles. How can we tell which miracles are of God, of Satan, and which are from other sources, such as self-induced or by trickery?

Scripture says even non-believers doomed for Hell can work healings and miracles. Judas, whom Jesus called the *"son of perdition"* (John 17:12), presumably worked healings and miracles along with the other 11 apostles and 70 other disciples, as noted in Matthew 10 and Luke 10. The other apostles failed to suspect for a moment that Judas was outside of their own kindred spirit. Also, Matthew 7:22-23 makes it clear that hell-bound sinners can preach the good news, cast out demons, and even work healings and miracles in the name of Jesus Christ.

✦

Many will say to me in that day, Lord, Lord, have we not prophesied in thy name? And in thy name have cast out devils? And in thy name done many wonderful works? And then will I profess unto them, I never knew you: depart from me, ye that work iniquity.
Matthew 7:22-23 (KJV)

✦

This poses a small dilemma for us of all faiths. If the Holy Spirit is still endowing people with the ability to work supernatural wonders, can God be working supernatural healings and miracles among those with false doctrines?

Judas, however, did not have any false doctrines. He hung around Jesus, the source of all sound teachings. Yet, he failed to accept Jesus as Lord of his life. Instead, he opted to join the Lord's band of followers for prestige, power, and position. Judas' doctrines were solid, but his motives were based on personal gratification.

The hell-bound sinners identified in Matthew 7:23 also were not noted for propagating any false teachings. They just had "wicked" intentions. To resolve this dilemma of can or will the Holy Spirit allow men to work godly healings and miracles while adhering to false doctrines, the answer is a resounding NO.

Consider this, if the Holy Spirit was behind the numerous and various miracles claimed by the Catholics wouldn't that validate and justify Catholic doctrines, especially those attributed to the Blessed Virgin Mary? Yes, it would. Augustine (AD 354–430), who is very much revered in the Roman Catholic Church, made the statement that the connection of alleged miracles with erroneous doctrines invalidates their claim to be genuine works of God.

Does this mean those holding to any false teachings cannot lay claim to supernatural healings and miracles from God? What about having any prayers answered by God? Do all of our doctrines need to be perfect before God answers our prayers or allows for supernatural wonders to be displayed?

A continuationist would believe that God can do anything He wants, and could easily restore an amputee's limb for anyone who honestly prayed with the required amount of unwavering faith. On the opposite side, a cessationist would say God would not restore an amputee's missing leg even if the most fervent prayer warrior prayed such a petition. Such a miracle would be outside of God's will for this day and age. Such supernatural wonders have been suspended until we see the two witnesses depicted in Revelation 11 show up on the world's scene.

It is obvious throughout Scripture that supernatural wonders were worked by those whose doctrines were closely in line with God's truth, though the miracle workers might have had lapses in judgment at times. Moses, Joshua, Elijah, Elisha, Isaiah, Gideon, Samson, and the Lord's apostles and disciples all worked supernatural wonders. These men were prophets, judges, apostles, and other special emissaries appointed by God.

Satan has no qualms about working his "lying wonders" to deceive anyone and everyone through whatever means he can devise, be it miracles, healings, magic, trickery, deception, or twisting of Scripture. He goes as far as God allows him to. Since God is omniscient, omnipotent, omnipresent, and infinite while Satan is finite, Satan's only recourse is to attack the zenith of God's creation, mankind. God seems to give Satan every opportunity to defeat His purpose for man, and He allows these attacks, but within limits and restrictions.

Satan can quote Scripture correctly as we have noted previously in this chapter, and he can appear as an "angel of light" to deceive the gullible and naïve as noted in 2Corinthians 11:14. Even demons can tell the truth and render praise to God. Luke 4:41 depicts Jesus casting out demons from a group of people, and they were not shy about shouting to the crowd, *"Thou art Christ the Son of God."*

We are still obligated to prove all things (1Thessalonians 5:21) and to discern the spirits (1John 4:1), and we must search out the truth in light of Scripture, not after someone's experiences or prophecies. The source of all sound doctrine is derived from Scripture, and Scripture alone. Few would argue this. The key question to ask is do we have the right interpretation of Scripture?

Some might ask why stir the mud? If supernatural healings, miracles, prophecies, and gifts of the Holy Spirit are still possible today, then non-Pentecostal churches need to teach and exercise them to reap the full benefits of God's grace. If, however, supernatural healings, miracles, prophecies and gifts of the Holy Spirit have passed away, then Pentecostal-type churches need to cease and desist teaching false doctrines and working false miracles so they can reap the full benefits of God's grace. If we do not resolve this issue, then confusion reigns within and without the Church.

Main Arguments. The main arguments for us today then become some of the following:

- Are miracles the same today as those recorded in the Gospels and Acts?
- Are only providential miracles occurring today? In other words, are there any supernatural miracles?
- Are there no miracles, supernatural or providential, being performed today?
- Are all gifts of the Holy Spirit available today?

- Have only the sign gifts (i.e., prophecies, healings, miracles, tongues, word of knowledge/wisdom) passed away?
- Are all gifts of the Holy Spirit obsolete today?

Now, which arguments are correct, and how can we tell? We also should consider who are the most vulnerable to false teachings on healings and miracles? Is it the youth, the unlearned, the emotionally crippled, or the physically handicapped? And, when we seek after sound doctrine, we also have to explore how our emotions and experiences play into our discernment process.

Emotions. Our emotions are God-given, and like our flesh and even our intellect, our emotions are sin-tainted. It has been said that emotions are indicators like an oil light on the car dash – do we have a problem or not? Emotions should not lead or confirm our decision process. This can be seen in the passage, *"Be angry and sin not"* (Ephesians 4:26), and *"love your enemies"* (Matthew 5:43). We may not feel like loving an unlovable or a despicable individual, but we are biblically commanded to love them with an action-based, sacrificial "agape" love.

Mormons, like Pentecostals and Charismatics, also believe in receiving some kind of affirmative feelings or "manifestation of the truth" to confirm their beliefs. In the Book of Mormon, for example, Moroni 10:4 states the following, *"And when ye shall receive these things, I would exhort you that ye would ask God, the Eternal Father, in the name of Christ, if these things are not true; and* ***if ye shall ask with a sincere heart, with real intent, having faith in Christ, he will***

manifest the truth of it unto you, by the power of the Holy Ghost." Mormons also speak in tongues much like Pentecostals and Charismatics. Mormons may claim to be Christians, but since they believe that Jesus is a brother of Lucifer, and any righteous person can eventually develop into an omniscient and omnipotent God, they fail to meet the basic criteria for being within the Christian camp. I mention the Mormon faith to highlight their similarities with the false teachings of Pentecostalism, especially in regards to the charismata.

Worshiping God in Spirit and Truth. Some believe worshiping God in the Spirit involves the emotions and/or speaking in tongues. A better interpretation of worshiping God in the Spirit involves being holy as He is holy, and being righteous and just, which are the foundations of His throne (Psalms 89:14). If we couple God's holiness, which is imputed to us, along with the truth of sound doctrine, then we are able to worship God in both spirit and truth as He desires.

Experiences. Experiences are a major element of our faith. Every answered prayer is an experience from God. To be disciplined by God is also an experience. These experiences help us stay true and grow. But good experiences can also be from Satan since he appears as an angel of light to deceive. Hence, we are commanded to discern all things (1Thessalonians 5:21).

With seven billion people in the world, whose experiences would you trust in for eternal truth? Jesus said, *"Be not deceived by Satan"* (Revelation 12:9), *"Be not deceived by anyone"* (2Thessalonians 2:3), and *"Do not deceive yourself"*

(1Corinthians 3:18)." So, even our own experiences have to be proven as well.

This author got into a seemingly friendly discussion one time over some doctrinal issues with a Pentecostal pastor. The discussion started off cordially enough, but as we progressed I noticed he was getting agitated and he could not defend his position from a biblical perspective. We weren't even talking about miracles, but about the biblical validity of having female pastors, elders, and deacons. Even a basic doctrine such as who is qualified to be an elder or deacon is often trivialized by Pentecostal churches. They justify their position by emphasizing we are all equal at the foot of the cross. Anyway, within 30 minutes our discussion abruptly ended with him closing his Bible and stating emphatically, "I don't want to hear anymore." He did not change his beliefs after our challenging Bible study, but instead, opted to cling to his experiences – "I know what I have seen and I know what I have experienced from the Lord. They confirm my stance."

In the end, most people believe what they want to believe because of their preconceived assumptions and biases. Most Catholics stay Catholics, Muslims stay Muslims, Baptists stay Baptists, and Pentecostals stay Pentecostals. Few venture away from the faith they were raised in.

That is why it takes an act of God at times as 2Timothy 2:25 says, "*if God peradventure*" (KJV), to get us or a loved one away from false teachings. This is especially true if false teachings are experience-based. Why? Because we think to ourselves, God would not allow ME to be deceived, or God would not give ME a stone or a snake if I asked for bread.

In reality, if someone gets tangled up in some false teachings it is because they eventually accept the "itching ear" syndrome or the warm emotional feelings, or the flash and bang of the miraculous. If it sounds good, feels good, and looks good, at least on the surface, it must be good – so they think. By chasing after the lusting of their own heart and feel good feelings, they, thereby, leave the protection God affords through sound teachings.

Peter said in 2Peter 1:20 that *"no prophecy of Scripture is a matter of one's own interpretation."* In other words, our interpretation of Scripture is not based on subjective personal experiences, but on objective, evidential, and substantiated facts. Unfortunately, many in the Pentecostal/Charismatic camps prefer to put their Bibles on the shelf and trust what experiences or visions emanates from themselves or their favorite preacher or teacher. The more bizarre the experience the more reliable it is to them. Truth becomes whatever happens to them and becomes self-evident. No proving of their experiences is required since they automatically believe they are directly from God.

Every one of us, however, is encouraged to experience God. Psalms 34:8 states it this way, *"O taste and see that the LORD is good."* Peter says if we are saved we have experienced or *"tasted the kindness of the Lord"* (1Peter 2:3).

Only the works of Jesus and the apostles are we ever commanded to evaluate and assess their validity as from God. The determining factor was their ability to violate or suspend a natural law. In other words, many of their healings and miracles were supernatural. For everyone else we are commanded to evaluate their fruit and not their works. *"You shall know them by their fruits"* (Matthew 7:16). Being filled with the Spirit should produce fruit of the Spirit, not the gifts of the Spirit. The key fruit being our love for each other (John 13:35) and our ability to dwell in unity (John 17:35), with the other fruit being joy, peace, patience, kindness, goodness, faithfulness, gentleness, and self-control (Galatians 5:22).

Pentecostalism has been phenomenally successful in attracting converts, but has failed horrendously in maintaining unity. Henri Gooren of the IIMO Research Centre, The Netherlands, states that "Pentecostal flexibility and adaptability are the keys to its success, but also the keys to its fragmentation and division. Where the Spirit flows freely, schisms happen frequently as dissident leaders break off to start their own churches. These dynamic religious entrepreneurs make Pentecostalism flexible and successful—and highly fragmented. The result is schism and contention and in the subsequent abrasions quite a number retire hurt and disillusioned. This issue explains the high drop-out rates in Pentecostal churches, especially in developing countries."[4] But this disunity only confirms that the Holy Spirit is not working in their midst as Pentecostals claim He is.

Pentecostals and Charismatics always seem to be looking for something bigger and better with more flash and bang. If they don't find that next experience, they begin to doubt their faith and wonder what is wrong. It seems their faith is like a drug, where they have to up the dosage over time to either keep the high going or to find that elusive instantaneous fix for one or more of their problems. This is probably why we

---

[4]http://www.arsdisputandi.org/publish/articles/000173/index.html

have seen Pentecostalism morph into at least three distinct waves or movements over the past 100 years. Unfortunately, instead of evolving into a movement more closely aligned with the Scriptures, each subsequent wave has become known for their more bizarre behavior and abhorrent teachings.

On a sobering note, Hebrews 6:4-6 gives us a warning about those who do experience God's goodness and then reject it – *"For in the case of those who have once been enlightened and have tasted of the heavenly gift and have been made partakers of the Holy Spirit, and have tasted the good word of God and the powers of the age to come, and then have fallen away, it is impossible to renew them again to repentance."* This passage is not alluding to someone being able to lose their salvation, but of an unsaved person rejecting what the clear teaching and godly experiences they might have witnessed while in a bible-believing environment.

Doctrinal Statements. Virtually all churches provide statements of their doctrinal positions for review by inquisitive visitors and congregants. These doctrinal statements are quite helpful to quickly assess whether someone can make a church their church home. As an example, the Southern Baptist Faith & Message provides descriptions of its core doctrinal teachings. Of particular and relevant interest is their description of the functions of the third person in the Trinity, God the Holy Spirit.

"The Holy Spirit is the Spirit of God, fully divine. He inspired holy men of old to write the Scriptures. Through illumination He enables men to understand truth. He exalts Christ. He convicts men of sin, of righteousness, and of judgment. He calls men to the Savior, and effects regeneration. At the moment of regeneration He baptizes every believer into the Body of Christ. He cultivates Christian character, comforts believers, and **bestows the spiritual gifts by which they serve God through his church**. He seals the believer unto the day of final redemption. His presence in the Christian is the guarantee that God will bring the believer into the fullness of the stature of Christ. He enlightens and empowers the believer and the church in worship, evangelism, and service."

I emphasized the statement where the Holy Spirit "**bestows the spiritual gifts by which they serve God through his church.**" Nowhere in the Baptist Faith and Message are the gifts of the Holy Spirit defined. This loose definition allows each local church body to exercise the appropriate gifts defined in the scriptures as they deem fit.

Some would accuse this inclusivity as making the Southern Baptist a liberal organization. Being inclusive of cessationist and continuationist viewpoints actually allows Southern Baptist fellowships to position themselves extremely well to accommodate people of both persuasions within its walls. The harmony and unity experienced by so many Southern Baptist churches with such a doctrinal diversity is a testimony to the world of the love they have for each other and the movement of the Holy Spirit within their midst to help maintain their unity. God has used such unity to make the Southern Baptist not only one of the largest church denominations but also the largest mission-sending organizations in the world.

Southern Baptists have within their ranks people self-labeled as "bapticostals." Bapticostals are those who believe in the continuance of the gifts of the Holy Spirit. Basically, it is the lingering effects of the charismatic influence from the 1960s. John Piper, a calvinistic Baptist preacher and author, is also a renowned advocate for the charismata in today's churches.[5] With a resurgence of the "Reformed" or calvinistic teachings within the Southern Baptist churches in recent years this is quite understandable.

Calvinism in its truest sense, as can be gleaned from John Calvin's (1509-1564) own writings in his Institutes, is predominantly feelings-based. For example in book 1, chapter 7, section 5 (or 1.7.5) Calvin states, "We can FEEL completely sure that God's word is true…we FEEL a divine energy" (emphasis by the author). According to his Institutes, in book 3, chapter 2, section 6, Calvin claims that our salvation is based on what we realize, visualize or experience. And in section 14 he states, "This knowledge (need for faith) is far superior: the human mind has to go out of and beyond itself to reach it." In section 19, he claims "God is far away from us and He must be discerned."

In response to this, James 4:8 contradicts what Calvin wrote, by stating that we are to draw near to God (through humbled obedience) and He will draw near to us. God, therefore, is not as far away from us as Calvin claims.

The ability to discern God seems to be more of Calvin's esoteric or mystical belief system (we must "feel" God and the "human mind has to go out of and beyond itself to reach it"). Calvin also placed excessive esoteric meaning to the

---

[5]http://sovgracenc.org/2013/11/john-piper-on-the-charismatic-movement/

sacraments. For example, he believed communion was spiritual food able to keep people alive physically (see Institutes 4.2.1 and 4.17.1). Calvin eventually claimed that communion is a mystery that he feels, but does not understand (see Institutes 4.17.31-32); but that is more from his entrenched holdover from his early upbringing as a Catholic.

One more point on Calvinism. Many Calvinists see their faith as being very intellectually driven. After all, Calvin even makes the statement in 3.2.15 that "faith is SURE and CERTAIN" (emphasis by the author). According to Scripture, however, faith is not fact, so it cannot be absolutely sure and certain on this side of Heaven since it is not yet realized. Faith, remember, is based on the "*assurance of things hoped for, the conviction of things not seen*" (Hebrews 11:1). We may have a personal conviction that our faith is rock solid, but in its truest form, our faith, though not being a blind faith, is a substantiated, evidential faith based on the confirmation of Scriptures being absolutely truthful.

Faith is also temporal or earthly, and it will be done away with once we transfer to Heaven. Even Calvin expressed concern about his "SURE" faith, which, if you recall from his statement above, is actually based on feeling that God's word is true (Institutes 1.7.5). His concern is seen in his statement that "there is hardly anyone (of the elect) who does not think sometimes 'If my salvation comes only from God's election, what proof have I of that election?' [There is none!] When this thought dominates an individual, he will be permanently miserable, in terrible torment or mental confusion" (Institutes 3.24.4).

What a sad state of those who believe in election the way John Calvin articulates it! If faith was SURE & CERTAIN as he stated in Institutes 3.2.15, why should there be any doubt? But that is the ultimate outcome of a feelings-based religious system –despair. These opinions of Calvin, which are not based on Scripture, are very esoteric, mystical, or feelings-based. When devotees of a feelings-based religious system such as Calvinism, Pentecostalism, and Mormonism finally comprehend that their faith is based on their up and down feelings and not on substantiated evidence, which God has amply provided as found in His word and in the resurrection of Christ, despair will eventually set in, until they can get their next emotional lift.

In contrast, our Judeo-Christian faith should not be a blind faith as all other religions are, but a faith based on credible and substantive evidence. This substantiated evidence is especially highlighted in Acts 17:3 where Paul was *"explaining and giving evidence that the Christ had to suffer and rise again from the dead."* God has even given sufficient natural evidence to the unbelieving masses as is seen in Romans 1:19-20. None of us with normal intelligence will have a valid excuse that we didn't know these things.

"Because that which is known about God is evident within them; for God made it evident to them. For since the creation of the world His invisible attributes, His eternal power and divine nature, have been clearly seen, being understood through what has been made, so that they are without excuse." Romans 1:19-20.

Southern Baptists have, unfortunately, even devoured teachings by Henry Blackaby and Claude King ("*Experiencing God*"), which strongly convey the Holy Spirit speaks to individuals directly these days. In essence, their teachings convey we can receive direct communication from God just like King David, Gideon, Joshua, and the Apostles. In their "*Experiencing God*" workbook, to extract one example, they make this statement in Unit 7, The Crisis of Belief section: "Before you call yourself, your family, or your church to exercise faith, be sure you have heard a word from God."[6]

If someone has a definitive word from God, then why is faith needed? Just move out on fact! All this esoteric or mystical, feelings-based sensing of God results in subjective, extra-biblical words from the Lord, which are not from Him at all, and are becoming more and more commonplace even within once staunch conservative-leaning churches.

When Abraham was specifically and directly told by God to sacrifice his son, Isaac, there was no faith involved. It was fact since he had direct, non-subjective, communication with God. When Moses was directly commanded by God to migrate the Hebrews from Egypt to the Promised Land, he, too, was going on fact, not faith. There was no subjectivity to the commands. The same could be said about Elijah, Elisha, Joshua, and King David. They had in some form or fashion the ability to receive unequivocal, undeniable, communications from God. Now Moses and the other servants of the Lord did have to exercise faith in God.

[6] Henry T. Blackaby and Claude V. King, *Experiencing God* (Lifeway Press, Nashville, 1990, 113

Hebrews 11:24 plainly states that, *"By faith Moses, when he had grown up, refused to be called the son of Pharaoh's daughter."*

In times past, God worked empirically with these early prophets, servants, and kings. We also have to consider that these "fathers" and prophets were held to a higher accountability than what we are today. For us, communication with God is considerably different. As Hebrews 1:1-2 says, *"God, after He spoke long ago to the fathers in the prophets in many portions and in many ways, in these last days has spoken to us in His Son."* Today, our communications with God is more subjective, and not as empirical.

When someone says they received a direct word from God there is no way to prove that to be so. We would have to take their word on blind faith, which is not scriptural. Sad to say, when someone says that God told them to kill their children, (and such situations have occurred several times in recent years) and they drowned or shot their children, how is that different from someone in church proclaiming a word from the Lord? There is no difference. Neither one of them can be proven to be truly of God. Their statements can only be accepted on blind faith or totally disregarded as internally contrived.

How does God talk to His people today through His Son? God speaks to us through His word today, and His word, as found in the 66 books of the Bible, is available to everyone. We have a level playing field. Young and old, male and female, free and slave can all discern God's word for their particular situation. For example, wives are to submit themselves unto their own husbands (Ephesians 5:22); husband are commanded to love their wives as Christ loved the Church (Ephesians 5:25); and children are to obey their parents (Ephesians 6:1). It's odd that every one of us have trouble keeping these simple commandments. Why then would God go out of His way to give people additional words, commands, and prophecies if we don't follow the obvious commands and principles in His word?

Can we "sense" God's leading in our lives today? Yes, we can sense God's leading, but it should never be by our feelings or by our five physical senses. Our five physical senses of sight, smell, hearing, touch, and taste cannot perceive God in our day and age since He is spirit and we are flesh. Our feelings or emotions only come into play after our intellect comprehends a particular truth or falsehood.

For example, if we are out late at night in a strange part of town and we see some hooded young people coming in our direction we might consider a few responses. Our intellect processes the information received from our five senses such as seeing cocky behavior, hearing coarse talk, and smelling alcohol or marijuana – and we then respond by fighting or fleeing, with our emotions giving our bodies signals of at least agitation, nervousness, and fear. But those signals could be totally erroneous. Those hooded young people could be teenagers leaving church and talking about the day's events while cleaning up beer bottles around their church building.

Another example is when someone receives the gospel message through seeing, hearing, or even touching (e.g., Braille), and their intellect processes the information; thereby giving them the comprehension of its truthfulness. Varying emotions may well up such as remorsefulness over sinful behavior and joy over prospects of receiving eternal life. Or, if someone is antagonistic toward the gospel message, they may become agitated, angry, and even combative. In either case, an intellectual decision to accept or reject the gospel message as true becomes paramount – not based on their feelings, but based on the intellectual comprehension of the information. Feelings are not, or should not be, a leading indicator in our decision process, but a lagging indicator.

Remember, the Holy Spirit is out to transform our sinful character first by renewing our minds (Romans 12:2 and Ephesians 4:23), and not our feelings or five physical senses. After our mind or intellect is renewed then our feelings and senses will naturally follow.

Also, remember the Holy Spirit is the Spirit of truth. He was instrumental in authoring God's word, the Bible, and as Ephesians 5:9 states, the fruit of the Spirit is in all goodness and righteousness and truth. Our faith comes by hearing or comprehending the word of God (Romans 10:17) and not by feeling it or sensing it.

Pentecostals have it backwards when they focus on the feelings or heart aspects of believing, hoping, and trusting. The common thread that ties our faith, our hope, our love, and our trust in God together is not our feelings or senses, but the evidential and substantiated truth of God's word, which is first intellectually comprehended.

Have you noticed whatever the world focuses on it is diametrically opposed to the word of God. James the elder strongly labeled the readers of his epistle as "*adulteresses*" for they failed to realize, to know, in essence to understand "*that friendship with the world is hostility toward God*" (James 4:4). The world says it is okay to do whatever feels good, and to follow your feelings.

Pentecostals also say it is okay to trust your feelings, or your heart, and not your intellect. They virtually subscribe to the mantra depicted in the Stars Wars Trilogy "Use the Force, Luke," where the force is some mystical entity that can be tapped into with feelings, with incantations in the name of Jesus, or by giving "seed" money to ministries. These multi-million dollar ministries should live by their own advice that they give to their donors and pray to the Lord for direct infusion of funds. Why do they rely on donors? Because their donors are gullible and will easily give "seed" money with the hope of receiving free cash or free health after they give.

The Bible, however, says just the opposite. We are to know, understand, comprehend what the will of the Lord is (Ephesians 5:17); and we can even know or comprehend that we have eternal life (1John 5:13). Not feel, assume, guess, or sense, but to know or mentally comprehend these things. Our knowing, our understanding, our comprehension begins with our intellect and not with our five physical senses or emotions.

When Scripture commands us to love God, to love one another, to love our spouses, and to love our enemies, it is not with a feelings-based love, but with an action-based love. This love is called "agape" in Greek, and it involves our intellect driving our actions, not our feelings driving actions. When Jesus died for the world, He had an agape-type of love for us. If His love was feelings-based, He would not have sacrificed Himself for the unlovable creatures we can be at times.

When our intellectually-driven actions are proper and biblical, our feelings will naturally follow. But whenever our feelings take the lead in forming our decisions and actions we are doomed to error. How many times have you heard Pentecostals say "stop trusting in your mind, but feel the presence of God?" One Pentecostal told me that I relied on doctrine too much, and I should just let go and have my feelings and my heart take over. Therein lays the core problem with Pentecostalism and why they are so prone to deception.

SHOULD WE MIRROR THE CHURCH OF ACTS?

One of the key arguments from Pentecostals is that the New Testament Church should mirror the early Church as found in Acts in all aspects, to include working of supernatural miracles, the continuance of visions and dreams, and the continuance of all the gifts of the Holy Spirit.

The key question then becomes do we still have apostles, men like Peter and Paul, running around today? If true apostles still exist, then the Bible should still be growing since they could easily pen and confirm Scripture. But if apostles have truly ceased, we have to acknowledge certain other events in Acts will be unrepeatable in subsequent generations.

True enough, the modern church does mirror the early church in one very important aspect. We often too easily accept false teachings on face value as readily as they did. Jesus, as well as all the writers of the New Testament, constantly challenged their listeners and readers on the dangers of letting in heretical teachers and teachings. One of the crucial indicators of spotting heretical teachings is often discovered after the damage is done because the ruse is so close to the genuine article. We have to remember the words of Jesus in Matthew 7:16, *"You shall know them by their fruits."*

Most Pentecostals (or continuationists) actually acknowledge that true apostles have ceased and the miracles of today are not the same as they were back then, though they still believe all gifts of the Holy Spirit are available for the Church today. There is an element, however, of the 3rd Wave movement that is trying to establish itself with apostolic credentials. As of 1999, they have even formed the International Coalition of Apostolic Leaders.[7] New apostles were once able to join by paying $69 a month as membership dues. No testing or validation of apostolic credentials were required other than the ability to pay $69.

Prove All Things. To discern whether or not certain "miraculous" events are of God or of Satan or of self or of nature we must do some due diligence. We must be like the Bereans in Acts 17 who searched the Scriptures daily to determine the truth. If an event lacks credibility we are not obligated to believe that it came from God. Recall that most miracles of Jesus and His apostles and disciples were available for all to examine closely – they were not subjective, but substantiated.

In John 9:18-19 the Jews did not believe the blind man that Jesus healed had been blind from birth and had recently received his sight, until they called his parents in to question them, saying, "*Is this your son, who you say was born blind? Then how does he now see*?" Other objective miracles can be found in

---

[7]http://www.coalitionofapostles.com/

Acts. In fact, Acts 4:16 quotes the Jewish leaders stating that "*a noteworthy miracle* [of a lame man] *has taken place through these men is apparent to ALL who live in Jerusalem, and we* [the skeptical Pharisees & Sadducees] *cannot deny it*." Jesus may have started his ministry in some secrecy ("*tell no one*"), but once He got going all of his healings and miracles as well as those of His apostles and disciples were available for all to validate and verify.

Is it possible to prove every incident of a so-called miracle? For providential or subjective miracles, no, it is not possible. It is like trying to put your thumb on a drop of mercury – it just squirts away from the pressure or scrutiny. To illustrate, one time after church a member asked me if I could lay my hands on his car and pray for it to start – and he was very serious. The car's battery had apparently failed, and no amount of jumping it with another car's battery had been successful.

This man and his wife and four children lived very frugally, so their car was an older model, and the battery was probably at the end of its service life. I offered to go and buy a new battery for them, but he wanted me to pray over the car so they could head home for dinner. I reminded him that I did not believe God would answer with a supernatural miracle so he better call for someone else who leaned more in that direction. He said to me, "Rod, I've noticed that whenever you pray, God answers." So how could I say no to such a compliment?

I put my hands on the car, and said a very simple prayer – "Lord, you know the situation we have here, and we humbly rely on you to resolve the problem with the car, and we will give you the glory." Sure enough, the car started on the first crank. He looked at this incident as an instantaneous miracle, and I looked at it as a normal process for a battery to typically recover some charge as the outside temperature warms up and as one other car tried to jumpstart the battery earlier – and it just so happened it was enough to allow the engine to start. God still gets the glory anyway. God knew when that battery was going to die and who needed to help a brother in need. Oh, and the battery was replaced later in the week. If it was a supernatural miracle then that battery should have lasted much, much longer, and I would be inundated with requests to restart other dead batteries. Uhm, I wonder if I can make money on that.

It wasn't but a year or so later when the battery and alternator in my own car gave out at the most inappropriate time on a heavily traveled city bridge during morning rush hour traffic. Why me, Lord? I was a faithful servant, a Sunday school teacher, a youth worker, a faithful husband and father, a church deacon in good standing, and a sacrificial giver. Shouldn't all that count for something? I am sure Job asked similar questions, and he did a similar self-evaluation, presumably, to make sure no sin was preventing the reception of timely blessings from God.

No amount of praying in Jesus' name got my car running again on that particular day, though I had confidence I was in God's will at the time. I can say this, God did answer my prayer for a timely and safe resolution since a friendly stranger gave me a lift off of the bridge and got me back home, and a quick call to a toll truck operator got the car to a repair shop without causing an incident on that accident-prone bridge. What did I learn that fateful day? God's word is still solid and can be trusted. God always gives His children teaching moments.

We just have to realize, like Job, God is going to test us constantly, and He is going to teach His children whether we want to be taught or not. Any stubbornness just slows the process down. Every one of us needs to learn each lesson quickly, correct any problems, and move on to the next situation, because God tries us "every moment."

⁂

What is man that You magnify him, and that You are concerned about him, that You examine him every morning and try him every moment? Job 7:17-18

⁂

We also may need to change our current materialistic mind set of "I want it now" to God's mind set of being patient and faithful in our Christian walk. There are no guarantees God will bless any of us materially or positionally, but at least we want to be in a position to be blessed. As Psalms 84:11b states, *"No good thing does He withhold from those who walk uprightly."*

Scripture is clear that God allows many of his faithful children to go through life with minimal possessions and minimal blessings. The widow with two mites in Mark 2:42-44 was as faithful as they come. She gave 100% of her income. She gave more than Bill Gates or Donald Trump has ever given. We can logically deduce she probably lived in abject poverty most of her years, and she probably died in that dire situation. Yet Jesus Christ highlighted her generosity above all others. Also, many destitute widows identified in 1Timothy 5 were to pray night and day for financial relief – and they were all noted for their godly faithfulness over the years.

We have biblical precedence showing that faithful followers of God do not always reap sufficient resources to comfortably survive on their own without help from family, friends, and even the church. God even allows some of His faithful servants to live a life of poverty. If you think about it, who is better to witness to the unsaved who are also in that condition than godly saints who are there living with and beside them. Therefore, God has His reasons for letting many of His saints live very frugal lifestyles. So, when name-it-and-claim-it advocates explain how we can control God for our benefit, they know neither the Scriptures nor the true power of God.

Also, we need to realize that sinful behavior does prevent God from blessing us at times. There is nothing worse than missing the blessings of God due to disobedience. Jeremiah mentions that sin actually prevents God's children from being blessed.

Your iniquities have turned these [blessings] away, and your sins have withheld good from you. Jeremiah 5:25

We should perform self-assessments when our prayers are not getting answered as we would expect. It could be, as a husband, that we need to treat our wife better for us to get more of our prayers answered (1Peter 3:7).

We also have to take note of Romans 11:35. According to this passage God owes us nothing. Even after being as faithful as the widows in 1Timothy 5 or as self-sacrificing as the widow with two mites, we are not owed the next breath we take – yet we owe God everything.

Or who has first given to [God] that it might be paid back to him again? Romans 11:35

Why doesn't God give people more compelling evidence? We must realize God only wants people in Heaven who want to be there, and He gives people convincing evidence, but not always compelling evidence – less they be forced to believe. Jesus' supernatural miracles and those of His apostles and early disciples were a temporal sign to Jesus' divinity and the Gospel's authenticity. Also, Jesus spoke in parables *"lest at any time they should see, hear, understand and should be converted"* (Mark 4:12) – in other words, be forced to believe.

Think about this – Jesus only appeared to believers following His resurrection and not to Pilate, or to Herod, or to the Pharisees and Sadducees, or to the soldiers who unmercifully scourged and crucified Him. While providential and subjective miracles still happen today, skeptics are free to claim coincidence or circumstantial. After all, such miracles do not break any known laws of nature. But when the two witnesses of Revelation 11 come on the world's stage, supernatural miracles will once more be used as a compelling sign to the soon return of the Messiah and of pending judgment.

CHAPTER 2
HEALINGS IN THE GOSPELS

"...And large crowds came to Him, bringing with them those who were lame, crippled, blind, mute, and many others, and they laid them down at His feet; and He healed them [ALL]..."
Matthew 19:2

The miracles of Christ are often categorized into four groups as 1) healings, 2) exorcisms, 3) resurrections, and 4) miraculous control over nature. Jesus is recorded to have performed about 11 miracles and 27 individual healings (which include exorcisms and resurrections). Scripture also records the apostles and disciples performing about another 20 healings and miracles (about half of what is recorded for Jesus).

Jesus, however, also worked countless other wonders as stated in John 21:25, *"And there are also many other things which Jesus did, which if they were written in detail, I suppose that even the world itself would not contain the books that would be written."* Particularly interesting from a miraculous perspective is Jesus' dealings with crowds of people that traveled to see Him for one reason or another.

Many study Bibles provide a listing of the miracles of Jesus and His apostles and disciples. Such a list is provided on the next two pages, but this list only identifies the individual healings and miracles and does not address the countless healings performed by Jesus whenever a crowd approached Him.

2. Healings In The Gospels

Jesus' Healings (27)	Matthew	Mark	Luke	John
1. Nobleman's son				4:46
2. Peter's mother-in-law healed	8:14	1:31	4:38	
3. Paralytic	9:2	2:3	5:18	
4. Impotent man healed				5:5
5. Withered hand	12:10	3:1	6:6	
6. Centurion's servant	8:5		7:2	
7. A lunatic child	17:14	9:26	9:38	
8. Issue of blood	9:20	5:25	8:43	
9. The daughter of a Syro-Phoenician woman	15:22	7:25		
10. Deaf and dumb healed		7:33		
11. Cleansing the leper	8:3	1:41	5:13	
12. Ten lepers			17:12	
13. Heals the woman with the spirit of infirmity			13:11	
14. Man with dropsy			14:2	
15. Malchus healed			22:51	
16. Blind men	9:27			
17. Blind men	20:30	10:46		
18. Blind man		8:23		
19. Blind man				9:1
20. Demoniac in the synagogue		1:26	4:35	
21. Demoniac	12:22		11:14	
22. Demoniac	9:32			
23. Raising Jarius' daughter	9:18	5:42	8:41	
24. Raising the widow's son			7:11	
25. Lazarus raised				11:43
26. His resurrection			24:6	10:18
27. Resurrections of countless saints	27:52			

Jesus' Other Miracles (11)	Matthew	Mark	Luke	John
28. Water changed to wine				2:9
29. Drought of fishes			5:6	
30. Feeding five thousand	14:15	9:41	9:12	6:5
31. Feeding four thousand	15:32	8:8		
32. Tempest stilled	8:26	4:39	8:24	
33. Walking on the sea	14:25	6:48		
34. Tribute money	17:24			
35. Cursing the fig tree	21:19			
36. Second drought of fish				21:6
37. Ascension to heaven		16:19		
38. Appearing to disciples	Matthew 14:14; 15:29-31			

Peter's Healings and Miraculous Wonders (5)	Acts
1. Lame man cured	3:7
2. Peter's shadow healed people	5:15-16
3. Aeneas	9:34
4. Dorcas raised from the dead	9:40
5. Ananias and Sapphira	5:5, 10

Paul's Healings and Miraculous Wonders (10)	Acts
6. Lame man cured	14:10
7. Damsel with the spirit of divination	16:18
8. Eutychus restored to life	20:10
9. Father of Publius healed	28:8
10. Everyone on the Island of Malta healed	28:9
11. Elymas blinded	13:11
12. Viper's bite	28:5
13. Paul & Barnabas worked signs & wonders	14:3
14. Paul's handkerchief worked miracles	19:11-12
15. Paul heals a lame man in Lystra	14:8-10

Miracles Performed by Others (5)	Acts
16. The seventy performed healings and exorcisms	Luke 10:17
17. Apostles worked signs and wonders	5:12
18. Stephen performed "great wonders and signs"	6:8
19. Philip performed healings, signs, and miracles	8:6-13
20. Ananias heals Paul of his blindness	9:17

HEALING THE CROWDS

The four Gospels and Acts mention crowds and multitudes of people more than 140 times. In fact, we will see that anyone and everyone who had an illness in these crowds were instantaneously healed either by Jesus or by His apostles and disciples. The Epistles, on the other hand, never address crowds of people being healed. What Jesus accomplished with the crowds is phenomenal. Thousands came to listen to Him (Luke 12:1) and be healed, and they ALL walked away healed of whatever ailments they had, with no exceptions, no failures, and no partial healings. This is a far cry from what we see today, where only a few "easy" cases ever seem to get healed.

The Gospel of Matthew records 10 incidences where Jesus healed everyone in a crowd who had a need for a healing. Mark records Jesus conducting healings within five crowds. Four of them are parallel passages to those recorded in Matthew, and the fifth could be considered unique to Mark. Luke also records Jesus working healings within six crowds. Again, four of them are parallel passages to those recorded in Matthew with two of them being unique to Luke. The Gospel of John records healings within only one crowed – the crowd of five thousand men, not counting women and children. This is the only miracle which is included in all four Gospels.

The following 10 sections take a brief look at the crowds of people identified in the Gospel of Matthew, and the healings received by anyone and everyone who was ill.

CROWD INCIDENT #1 – *Matthew4:23-24*

Jesus was going throughout all Galilee, teaching in their synagogues and proclaiming the gospel of the kingdom, and ***healing every kind of disease and every kind of sickness among the people****. The news about Him spread throughout all Syria; and they brought to Him all who were ill, those suffering with various diseases and pains, demoniacs, epileptics, paralytics;* ***and He healed them [ALL]****.*

The first incident where Jesus heals the sick and infirmed within a crowd occurs after He returns from being baptized by John the Baptist and spending 40 days in the wilderness. Earlier in Matthew 4 we see Jesus selecting four of His disciples – Simon Peter and his brother, Andrew, James and his brother, John, who were the two sons of Zebedee.

When Matthew stated that Jesus healed *"every kind of disease and every kind of sickness,"* this seems to be all inclusive of numerous diseases and pains, demoniacs, epileptics, paralytics, mutes, deaf, blind, lame, crippled, lepers, and probably a host of other ailments we can glean from any medical dictionary. There is no reason from the context of this and similar passages of Scripture to limit the types of ailments Jesus was capable of healing. This would be one of our assumptions. After all, if there were illnesses or ailments Jesus could not heal, then it would demolish His claim of being the Anointed One, the Christ, the Messiah, the Son of God who came in fulfillment of Scripture to give sight to the blind and set the captives free (Luke 4:18).

Another assumption we can glean from this passage is when verse 24 says that *"He healed them"* we can logically assume Jesus healed them ALL. All of the healings, per the context, would have been complete and instantaneous, which marks them as being supernatural. In other words, one or more laws of nature would have had to be broken. Even a simple paper cut needs time to heal, but Jesus circumvented time by healing everyone who needed a healing instantaneously, completely, and painlessly, with no bandages, no surgery, no medication, and no scarring.

Plus, there would not have been any exceptions or partial healings. If only "some" or "many" or "few" were noted to be healed we would then need more clarification to determine why He could not heal others. In such a case of anything less than 100% being healed instantly and completely would actually undermine the power and authority of Christ.

The very next verse, Matthew 4:25, reads that "*large crowds followed Him.*" How large were the large crowds? I think we can comfortably assume in the thousands, if not tens of thousands.

When the Bible records that Jesus fed 4,000 and then 5,000 men it was noted in both situations that the women and children were not counted. Assuming each family consisted of at least a husband, a wife, and one child, the crowds would have exceeded 12,000 and 15,000 respectively. Acts 2:41 and 4:4 also record 3,000 souls and 5,000 men coming to faith after hearing the Gospel presented.

Luke 12:1 states that "*after so many thousands (or 'myriads') of people had gathered together that they were stepping on one another.*" This passage, using the term for "myriads," indicates possibly more than 10,000 were listening to Jesus teach His disciples, since Luke used the same term the Apostle John used in Revelation 5:11. In that passage, John the Revelator tried to tally up the angels circling the throne of God – *"the number of them was myriads of myriads, and thousands of thousands."*

From this first crowd incident we clearly see Jesus healing 100%. He also healed every ailment instantaneously. We can also ascertain He worked supernaturally, not providentially – thereby, confirming His divine credentials. His reputation was soaring exponentially throughout the nation of Israel and surrounding jurisdictions.

Crowd Incident #2 – Matthew 8:16-17

When evening came, they brought to Him many who were demon-possessed; and ***He cast out the spirits with a word, and healed ALL who were ill.***

Earlier, in Matthew 8, we see again large crowds following Jesus as he came down a mountain from teaching His disciples. It was the Sabbath and Jesus took the opportunity to heal Peter's mother-in-law who had a fever. This miracle seemed rather trivial. After all, it was a simple headache or fever. Plus, it was a miracle of convenience, otherwise, Jesus and His disciples would have had to scrounge up their own meal that evening. As a side note, the Bible records Jesus performing seven healings on the Sabbath.

1. Peter's mother-in-law (Matthew 8:14-15; Mark 1:29-31)
2. Man with an unclean spirit (Mark 1:21-28; Luke 4:31-37)

3. Man with withered hand (Matthew 12:10; Mark 3:2; Luke 6:10)
4. Woman crippled by an evil spirit for 18 years (Luke 13:11-14)
5. Man with dropsy, possibly edema (Luke 14:1-4)
6. Crippled man at the pool of Bethesda (John 5:9)
7. Man born blind (John 9)

As the sun went down on that Sabbath day the people then came from all around the region to see Jesus, the 100% miracle worker. Matthew's passage emphatically states that Jesus *"healed ALL who were ill."* The parallel passage in the Gospel of Mark adds a different perspective. Mark 1:31 states that Jesus *"healed MANY that were sick."*

When does "all" mean all, when does "many" mean all, when does "some" mean all, and when does "all" mean some? In ALL cases, the meaning of ALL is context-dependent. For example, Romans 3:9 says *"…for we have before proved both Jews and Gentiles are ALL under sin."* In this case, ALL means everyone – Jew & Gentile, elect and non-elect, male and female, young and old.

In Romans 3:19, 23 we see that *"ALL the world may become guilty"* for *"ALL have sinned."* Here, ALL means everyone. In Romans 5:18, *"By one transgression there resulted condemnation to ALL, even so through one act of righteousness* [by Christ] *there resulted justification of life to ALL,"* we see that eternal life is made available to everyone. But it gets selective in Romans 10:12 where it is stated *"…the same Lord over ALL* [everyone] *is rich unto ALL* [or only those] *that call upon him.*

So, it is comfortably assumed when Mark stated that Jesus healed many he means to convey that Jesus healed ALL and there were many of them. This is seemingly confirmed when we see what Mark stated in 1:33 *"and the whole city had gathered at the door."*

Crowd Incident #3 – Matthew 9:26, 35

And the fame [of Jesus] went abroad into all that land…And Jesus went about all the cities and villages, teaching in their synagogues, and preaching the gospel of the kingdom, and ***healing every sickness and every disease*** *among the people."*

Again, there is no reason to limit what kinds of illnesses and diseases Jesus came across. After all, is there anything too hard for God? Absolutely not.

If you were to consider the people in your church you would probably see many people having typical ailments recognized throughout society. Some would have common colds, back aches, tooth aches, headaches, various viruses, and even poison ivy. Then there are the ailments of age or bad diets such as arthritis, hypertension, diabetes, Alzheimer's, prostate cancer, breast cancer, and other cancers. Then you can't forget about those with birth defects such as mental and physical handicaps. Another group of individuals deal with handicaps from accidents at work such as missing fingers or toes, amputated limbs, broken backs, and broken arms and legs. Did Jesus heal such variety of ailments? There is no logical reason to deny such healings by the Son of God.

King Herod the Great (c. 74–4 BC) had substantially completed the main part of the temple's rebuilding by the time of his death in 4 BC. According to Josephus (Antiquities 15.11.2) there were more than 10,000 laborers employed at one time. Since the building was not entirely finished until 63 AD, only seven years before the destruction of the entire Temple in 70 AD, more than likely there were still hundreds of laborers employed in ongoing maintenance and finishing projects during the time of Christ. When Jesus visited the Temple at the first Passover of his ministry, it was said that the place had by then been under construction for 46 years. With a colossal project such as this, it seems reasonable there would have been numerous on-the-job accidents and even deaths. After all, the size of the smaller stones weighed between two and four tons each. These stones could easily and severely injure or kill those transporting and working around, on top or in between them. Injuries could have included broken bones and backs, and even amputations of fingers, toes, and limbs. Jesus probably healed many injured workers, who were once the primary wage earners for their families.

What about the healing of frivolous or minor cosmetic issues such as baldness or being overweight or underweight, or having a bigger nose than a person would like? Are those true ailments that prevent people from working or living a productive life? We will see later that Jesus did not respond to frivolous requests.

Crowd Incident #4 – Matthew 10:1-9

"Jesus gave His disciples (including Judas) the ability to cast out demons, to raise the dead, and to ***heal every kind of disease and every kind of sickness.****"*

Mark 6:7 adds *"they were anointing with oil many sick people and healing them."*

and Luke 9:1-2 adds *"**they were healing everywhere**"*

and Luke 10:1-17 states*"...the Lord appointed seventy (70) also...[to]* ***heal the sick in every city****..."*

Jesus distributed His power not only to His 12 disciples but to 70 others as well, and they too could heal anyone and everyone of anything and everything, anytime and every time, anywhere and everywhere they went. Even Judas, the son of perdition, was presumably endowed with the same power as his peers since there was no suspicion of him being anything but a disciple in good standing.

So far we have only covered four passages out of the ten identified in Matthew where Jesus healed 100% of the people 100% of the time; and we see now that this power was passed on to others.

This begs a question. Is this power still available today? Some say yes, others no. For those who say 'yes' there is no evidence of anyone performing the healings as attributed to Jesus and His disciples, much less doing *"greater works than these."* And this begs a few more questions. If this power ceased, when did it cease, and for what reasons? Please keep reading. The answers to these questions are forthcoming.

Crowd Incident #5 – Matthew 12:15-16

"...Many followed Him, and ***He healed them all,*** *and warned them not to tell who He was."*
Mark 3:10-12 adds *"...Whenever the unclean spirits saw Him, they would fall down before Him and shout, 'You are the Son of God!' And He earnestly warned them not to tell who He was."*

There is a hermeneutic principle which says we should go with the parallel passage that provides clarification. Since Mark indicates that it was demons that Jesus commanded *"not to tell who He was"* we can see the application in Matthew.

Matthew 12:18-21 quotes from Isaiah 42:1-4. These two passages highlight that Jesus was to come with a low-key ministry ("...He *will not quarrel, nor cry out; nor will anyone hear his voice in the streets*"). Beginning with His humbled birth in a manger to being buried in a borrowed tomb, His life was designed for no wealth, no extravagance, and no sought after fanfare.

What a stark contrast with those in the Pentecostal healing and prosperity preaching forefront who travel in private jets, have luxurious multi-million dollar homes, and stay in posh hotels. Even the Lord's disciples were told not to acquire gold, or silver, or copper for their income as they traversed the countryside with the command to heal every sick person, cleanse the lepers, and cast out demons free of charge (Matthew 10:8-9).

It is interesting to note that early in Jesus' ministry He tried to minimize the marketing of His capabilities by telling people not to tell anyone. Back in Matthew 8 Jesus heals a leper and told him, *"See that you tell no one, but go, show yourself to the priest."* This apparently allowed Him to be about His primary mission – and that was to teach.

Healings and miracles were secondary in nature since they only offered a temporary earthly fix. His teaching ministry, however, impacted lives for all eternity. The contrast between Christ and modern-day faith healers is night and day. The primary mission of Christ was to preach the Gospel, while faith healers promote themselves through their perceived healings, and rarely do they speak of the Gospel message that calls for true repentance.

Crowd Incident #6 – Matthew 14:14

"And Jesus went forth, and saw a great multitude, and was moved with compassion toward them, and ***he healed [ALL] their sick****."*

This passage is the beginning of the infamous feeding of the 5,000. As noted previously, if you factor in the women and children, this crowd could easily exceed 15,000. Pastors frequently preach about the wonders of how Jesus fed so many with so little. This wonder was supposed to help wake the disciples up to the fact that Jesus was indeed God in the flesh, since only God can create things out of nothing. What you don't often hear from the pulpit about this passage is before Jesus fed the people, He healed all the sick within the crowd (verse 14). Again, this is the only miracle found in all four Gospels.

John 6:2 adds that the *"large crowd followed [Jesus] because they saw the signs which He was performing on those who were sick."* They looked at Jesus as a miracle-vending machine. Matthew 14:13, Mark 6:35, and Luke 9:12 describe the place of this mighty work as "secluded" or "desolate." There were no restaurants, and no restrooms or other amenities nearby. The people seemed so desperate to be healed of whatever ailment they or a family member needed they made the trek with their family in tow even under less than practical traveling conditions.

It is natural for everyone, believers and non-believers alike, to desire health and prosperity for themselves and for their loved ones. As Job 2:4 records, *"Satan answered the LORD and said, 'Skin for skin! Yes, all that a man has he will give for his life.'"* Yes, we would do almost anything, and give up almost anything to pursue a remedy which would restore our health or the health of a loved one.

If there ever was a religion that seemed to offer such benefits on this side of glory, there would be a rush on the merchandise, so to speak. That is exactly what is seen in Pentecostalism, but it is only fool's gold. People are stampeding to get this faith for the wrong reason – for what they can get out of it. Most want free food, free health, and free money, but God wants repentance and willing followers who love Him for Himself and not for what they can get out of Him.

Crowd Incident #7 – Matthew 14:35-36

"And when the men of that place recognized [Jesus], they sent word into all that surrounding district and ***brought to Him ALL who were sick****; and they implored Him that they might just touch the fringe of His cloak; and* ***as many as touched it were cured****."* Luke 6:19 adds, *"for power was coming from Him and* ***healing them ALL****.'*

By this time in the ministry of Christ He and His disciples could not hide. The Lord's reputation for healing 100% brought almost everyone out to either receive His touch or just to touch the fringe of His robe.

This is actually a gold nugget of a passage. There is more to the Jewish robe than just being an outer garment. There is rich symbolic meaning embedded in each fiber of this "cloak" or so-called prayer shawl.

The shawl was made as a visual reminder of God and His law. There was a blue thread woven from one length to the other. The blue color was representative of the sky and to be heavenly focused. One thread of each of the four-cornered tassels was to be a deep blue color to remind them of their duty to keep the law.

According to Jewish tradition, there were 39 windings in each tassel, which equates to the numerical value of the Hebrew words "the Lord is One" or Yahweh. There are 613 knots in every one of these tassels corresponding to the 613 laws in the Law of Moses. Three hundred sixty-five (365) were probations – "Thy shall not" and two hundred forty eight (248) were affirmations – "Thy shall."

The Jewish men wore this prayer shawl, also called a "Talith," all the time, not just at prayer. "Talith" contains two Hebrew words; TAL meaning tent and ITH meaning little. Thus, each man had his own "Little Tent" or "Little Closet." Acts 18:3 depicts the apostle Paul as a Jewish Pharisee, but also as a "tentmaker." Many believe he made Taliths or prayer shawls to supplement his income, and not tents to live in.

Matthew 6:6 tells us when we pray we should enter into our prayer closet. For Jews this occurred when the shawl was pulled over their heads. Matthew 23:5 highlights how the Pharisees considered the tassels as special marks of sanctity and sought to enlarge them to display their self-perceived higher level of righteousness.

Since the four windings on the four-cornered tassels correspond to the Holy Name of God, when holding or viewing or touching the tassels we are symbolically embracing the entire Word of God, all the commands of God, and the Name of God. We are, in essence, embracing God, Himself. In Mark 5:25-34 a woman with a bleeding disorder grabs the tassels of Jesus' shawl, believing by faith she would be touching God and God would respond by touching her back – and He did.

Another interesting aspect of this shawl is in Revelation 19:11-16 where we see a picture of the returning Lord with His name on His thigh while riding on a horse. In our "Greek" mindset we imagine a tattoo or something similar on the thigh of Jesus when he returns as "King of Kings, and Lord of Lords". The Hebrew perspective shows something more specific. Since the knots of the tassels on the four corners of a

Talith spell out the name of Yahweh; therefore, while riding a white horse on His return to earth, the braids/knots/tassels/fringes of Yeshua's Talith actually rest on one or both of His upper legs allowing His NAME to be seen where? On His thigh.

Finally, we see in Genesis 49:10-12 that the robe or possibly the prayer shawl of the one called Shiloh (or Christ) was stained with blood, and in Revelation 19:13 His robe is dipped in blood. This seems to show the once-placid prayer shawl, which was used to procure God's favor through prayer, now signifies God's wrath is come upon the world.

Crowd Incident #8 – Matthew 15:30-38

"And large crowds came to Jesus, bringing with them those who were ***lame, crippled, blind, mute, and many others; and He healed them [ALL]****. So the crowd marveled as they saw the mute speaking, the crippled restored, and the lame walking, and the blind seeing; and they glorified God"*

This passage depicts the feeding of 4,000 men, not counting women and children. Prior to feeding them Jesus once again healed all their sick. Assuming the crowd consisted of 4,000 families, all looking for a healing for at least one of their loved ones, it seems reasonable Jesus healed around 4,000 people, or about one sick person per family.

Another interesting aspect of this passage is the healing of "lame" and "crippled" individuals. What is the difference between lame and crippled?

Lame in Greek is “cholos,” while crippled is “kullos.” The words are somewhat synonymous with subtle differences, but when used together Jesus seems to be invoking a play on words for emphasis – cholos and kullos. The subtle difference for being lame (cholos) seems to convey someone with a bum or broken leg while crippled (kullos) seems to convey someone possibly missing a limb.

Another Greek word used for “crippled” is “anaperos,” which conveys “injured or bereft of some body member.” Luke 14:13 states, "*But when you give a reception, invite the poor, the crippled* <anaperos>, *the lame* <cholos>, *the blind."*

A unique peculiarity of all the recorded healings in the New Testament is that Jesus restored individuals to their previous pre-existing condition or to a normative state such as giving sight to the blind man in John 9 who was born blind. It is never explicitly recorded that Jesus ever fashioned and restored a missing limb, created and inserted an eyeball, increased the IQ of a mentally challenged person, or fixed the chromosomes of a Down Syndrome person. It is conceivable Jesus performed such acts of kindness and mercy since, again, John made mention that countless other wonders too numerous to mention were accomplished by Him (John 21:25).

Jesus did restore a man’s ear after it was cut off (Luke 22:50-51), but He did not have to create a new ear. In essence, with a simple touch, He reattached the man’s lobbed-off ear with surgical precision, which would have included instantaneously realigning and reattaching all the blood vessels, nerve conduits, cartilage, and layers of skin – all without using any stitches, antibiotics, or bandaging, or having any scarring. This, in itself, would be a supernatural miracle which only God could have performed since creative power was required. Nowhere in Scripture is it evident Satan has such capabilities, with the possible exceptions of appearing as a serpent in the Garden of Eden, and transforming the magicians' rods into snakes. If God allowed or allows Satan to mimic such a healing, it would still be labeled a "lying wonder" with a sole purpose to deceive and confuse people.

Jesus said in Matthew 18:8, "*If your hand or your foot causes you to stumble, cut it off and throw it from you; it is better for you to enter life crippled <kullos>; or lame <cholos>, than to have two hands or two feet and be cast into the eternal fire.*" Matthew 15:30 and 21:14 also record that the blind, the CRIPPLED and the LAME (same Greek words as in 18:8) came to Jesus, and He healed them. Both 'lame' and 'crippled' are synonymous, and seem to be used interchangeably in these passages as conveying the amputation of hands and feet.

Since Jesus healed "*every kind of disease and every kind of sickness*" as noted in Matthew 4:23-24, it is very conceivable Jesus did heal people instantaneously of broken or even missing limbs and, by extension, with mental handicaps, to possibly include Down Syndrome, if that ailment was prevalent at that time in history. This is one of the assumptions we can logically deduce.

Pentecostals have a tendency to claim a miracle on pure speculation or even wishful thinking. An illustration of this was when my youngest daughter was expecting her fourth child. One of her prenatal checkups came back with what is described as an "echogenic spot" on the baby's heart, which is a possible indicator for a Down Syndrome child. She made me a very proud dad when she told her doctor to "bring it on – we will accept difficult times from the hand of the Lord as well as good times." Considering an abortion was just not in her vocabulary. She, her husband, her parents, her in-laws, her church family and several other church families naturally prayed for a normal birth, but prayers also went up for God's will to be done even if a special-needs child was born to them. At her next prenatal checkup her tests showed normal. Our Pentecostal family members and friends latched onto this incident as a miracle where God cured the Down Syndrome gene in vitro (within the womb). In actuality, her previous test is known as a "false positive."

False positive indicators are all too common in the medical field, especially if the genetic tests are not done within very specific timeframes early in the pregnancy. Also, since nothing is too hard for God, if He can cure in vitro He can also cure outside of the womb just as easily, instantaneously, completely, and permanently. But we have no confirmed evidence He has ever cured a Down Syndrome whether inside or outside of the womb, at least since the time of Christ. So it would be wishful thinking to credit Him for something He did not do, and does not do, and has not done since the time of Christ. We can definitely give God the credit and the glory for allowing a child to be born whether it is "normal" or handicapped.

Crowd Incident #9 – Matthew 19:2

*"Large crowds followed Him, and **He healed them [ALL]**."*

Crowd Incident #10 – Matthew 21:14

*"And the blind and the lame came to Jesus in the temple, and **He healed them [ALL]**."*

⁂

Again, we can logically assume in these passages that Jesus healed ALL who needed a healing in these crowds of people. Since Jesus traversed around the countryside, the crowds were ever-changing. The Internet, social media, cell phones, radio, and television were not needed since word of mouth preceded Jesus entering a new territory. Whole towns would rush to Him, and He would dutifully heal each and every one that had an ailment no matter how small or how involved. Again, the healings would have been instantaneous. No medications were needed, no follow up visits, and no time was needed to heal. The healings by the Messiah broke the known laws of nature to restore full organic functionality from a fever to having someone walk out of his tomb.

One of my brothers, a chiropractor, called me and asked if I would drop by his office one day. It was February 2013, which was Breast Cancer Awareness month, and he was hosting a lunchtime seminar for his staff with a guest speaker who was describing the benefits of Thermal Imaging scans to help detect breast cancer. He asked me to stay for the presentation. The presenter stated that thermal imaging is not a replacement for mammograms but augments it.

Thermal imaging captures heat signatures from the body while mammograms use penetrating x-ray technology. Thermal imaging has identified cancers where mammograms failed to do so, and vice versa.

Several normal scans were presented and compared with abnormal scans, which showed more red and yellow hues reflecting hot spots of suspected cancer cells. The presenter highlighted one case of a lady who for ten years had suspicious mammograms. Her oncologist kept advising her to have a biopsy to be safe, and a follow-up visit after another six months. She was ready to have a double mastectomy to get out from all the anxiety she was living with, but a friend suggested she should try a thermal imaging scan first. Sure enough her scan showed hot zones from her neck down. The technician, not the doctor, ask her if she drank any diet sodas. The lady replied that, yes, she drinks a few each day. The technician recommended for her to redo the imaging scan the next day, but for the next 24 hours she was to drink only water. She came back the next day and had a normal thermal imaging scan.

So she headed back to her oncologist to schedule a mammogram, and she got the first normal mammogram ever in her 10 years taking them. Naturally she had some words with her oncologist. I can't say avoiding diet sodas will fix every abnormal thermal imaging scan or mammogram results, but I highlighted this case to show that claims of instantaneous cancer cures are not always what they seem to be. This woman was "cured" within 24 hours simply by changing her diet, and no prayers were known to have been involved.

Like the Israelites who were deceived by the Gibeonites because they did not check things out more thoroughly, we should not take things at face value. Just because some faith healer or notable TV personality claims a healing for cancer, we are still obligated to prove all things before we blindly accept it.

DID JESUS ALWAYS HEAL EVERYONE?

According to these 10 passages in Matthew we just looked at, everyone that sought Jesus out or came to one of his teaching seminars definitely got healed. What a stark contrast to modern faith healings where only a few functional ailments seem to get healed. Naturally, there are passages in the Bible that Pentecostals use to justify why their faith healers are not able to heal 100%.

"And He could do no miracle there except that He laid His hands on a few sick people and healed them, and He wondered at their unbelief." Mark 6:5-6

Some continuationist preachers have used this passage in Mark to justify why some sick people walk away without getting healed and why even Jesus possibly could not heal everyone He touched. But that is a horrible interpretation and misapplication of this passage. When we consider that Jesus healed anyone and everyone who sought Him out for any and every kind of ailment there is no way this passage can convey such a position when we consider the whole counsel of God. This passage does not mean Jesus lost His healing powers. Instead this passage alludes to people not coming out to get healed, with the exception of a few. Though, Jesus did not heal many in His hometown for their unbelief as seen in this passage and in Matthew 13:58, yet most of His miracles were done in unrepentant towns, as noted in Matthew 11:20 and Luke 10:13.

Another aspect we need to factor in when we compare how Jesus healed with how we see people healing today is His mode of operandi. Jesus used various means and methods, and ALL of his healings were instantaneous and complete. He never had to hit or knock anyone down to give them a much-needed healing.

Methods of Healing. Jesus healed with a touch or with a word. He healed large groups and he healed selectively (e.g., one man at the pool of Bethesda). He healed remotely such as the Roman centurion's servant and the Syro-Phoenician's daughter. Jesus healed the ungrateful as seen with nine out of ten lepers who failed to even say thank you. He healed when faith was weak (a lunatic boy), and even when there was no pretense of faith as evident of the widow's son at Nain where no one asked Jesus for the son to be restored to life. Naturally, Jesus took pleasure in healing when faith was apparent in a sick individual (*"your faith has made you well,"* Matthew 9:22). Please note, a more accurate translation is "your faith has saved you" – indicating that we do not have to work our faith into a frenzy to get something from God.

It is interesting to note the only time faith became an issue with healing is when the faith of the apostles was not mature enough to heal a demon-possessed (lunatic) boy as identified in Matthew 17:15. What do we hear when someone fails to get healed at a faith healing service? We hear that the problem is with the sick individual and not with the faith healer. But God puts the blame squarely on those who have been given the power from the Holy Spirit to work healings and miracles. If someone doesn't get healed it is the so-called faith-healer's problem. Again, the Pentecostals have this backwards, as is often the case.

John MacArthur documents in his book *Strange Fire* that internationally-acclaimed faith healer, Benny Hinn, during his healing services uses screeners to keep the terribly deformed, any children with Downs Syndrome, and amputees at a distance and away from the stage, and definitely out of sight of TV cameras.[8] If Hinn genuinely had the ability to heal, there would be no need for him to avoid those who had organic ailments. In fact, the worst cases would have front row seats instead of being ushered away from camera view.

Another aspect about Jesus is that He also healed for convenience sake. This is quite notable when He cured Peter's mother-in-law so she could get up and feed them (Matthew 8:14-15). We can see that Jesus readily healed the easy cases such as fevers, and the hard cases such as Lazarus being dead and entombed for four days.

Jesus also healed within the synagogue and outside of the synagogue. He healed out of compassion, He healed sinners, He healed believers, and He healed unbelievers as evident with the man born blind in John 9 and with all demoniacs. Jesus not only healed Jews, He also healed foreigners. In essence, Jesus healed ALL who came to him for a healing, and

[8] John MacArthur, *Strange Fire,* Nelson Books (Nashville, TN 2013), 173

then some – whether they had organic or functional ailments. Again, there were no exceptions or incomplete healings.

If there is a way for false teachers to misinterpret or misapply a passage of Scripture they will not only do so, but they will exploit it till it is nearly a standard and fully accepted as Gospel truth. For example, the three passages of Scripture where Jesus healed in a multi-step process are often used to justify why faith-healers claim it can take days, weeks, months, or even years before a sick person can receive and claim their healing. Yet, in none of these passages did it take more than minutes for the individuals to be fully and irrevocably healed.

John 9:6-7 deals with a blind man on whom Jesus put a mud pack on the man's eyes and then told him to go wash it off. The blind man in all probability knew that the pool of Siloam was nearby, and did not have to trudge a long distance across town. He washed as directed, and he fully received his sight. Mark 7:33 highlights the deaf mute Jesus healed by putting his fingers first into the man's ears and then touching the man's tongue with a mixture of saliva and dirt. The third passage, Mark 8:23-25, shows Jesus healing a blind man by first taking him outside of town, then spat into his eyes, then put His hands upon him and asked the man what he was able to see. Then, finally, Jesus put His hands upon the man's eyes for the complete healing.

There is no indication in Scripture that Jesus' power was compromised in any of these situations. Rather Jesus, being true to His mission, used these multi-step processes to teach His disciples spiritual lessons. For example, the context of Mark 8 deals with the partial blindness of the disciples to fully recognize who Jesus was. Even after Jesus fed the four thousand He had to ask them *"do you not yet understand?"* (verse 21). After Jesus healed the blind man, He asked His disciples who do you say that I am (verse 29). Like the blind man who vaguely saw men as walking trees, the disciples partially understand who Jesus was. God would need to do something more specific to each of their minds for the Lord's disciples to fully comprehend the truth, just as Jesus had to initially heal the inoperative eyeballs of the blind man along with his cognitive ability to recognize walking trees as men.

Jesus always dealt with people's intellect to get them to a decision-making point, and never manipulated their emotions to get them to make the right decision. Though, Jesus might have stirred people's emotions by His actions and words, such as calling the Scribes and Pharisees hypocrites (Matthew 15:7) and whitewashed tombs (Matthew 23:27). He did not manipulate them through their emotions. Each person was responsible for their own words and actions when they acted upon their emotions. For example, out of jealousy the Jewish leaders arrested and jailed the apostles (Acts 5:17-18).

Miraculous Happenings. From a miraculous perspective, Jesus worked miracles to show he had dominion over all aspects of life. He controlled the weather as noted by Him calming of the sea. He ruled over the laws of physics by walking on water, turning water into wine, and feeding 5000 and then 4000 families with no more than one kids-meal to start from just to show how He can accomplish plenty with any small offerings we give to Him.

Jesus ruled over the animal kingdom as demonstrated by two large catches of fish. He also ruled over the plant kingdom as demonstrated by the withering of a fig tree. Jesus even worked miracles for convenience sake by turning water into high quality wine at a wedding. He even had Peter catch a fish with money in it so their taxes could be paid. Finally, Jesus demonstrated his dominion over life and death by raising Jairus' daughter, the widow's son, His dear friend, Lazarus, and He even raised Himself from the dead as noted in John 2:19.

Resurrections. Here is an interesting aspect on the recorded resurrections within the Bible. The passage of the rich man in torment (Luke 6:19-31) clarifies no one from Hell makes it back out for a second chance since the rich man asked Abraham to send someone from paradise side to witness to his brothers. This seems to mean the ten resurrections recorded in the Bible were presumably all redeemed individuals, and half of them were children, with the very first recorded resurrection being that of a Canaanite boy who was not a Jew.

1. Elijah raised a non-Jew, the son of a Canaanite from Sidon, which was the birthplace of Jezebel (1Kings 17:17-24)
2. Elisha raised the Shunammite son (2Kings 4:32-37)
3. Elisha's remains restored a dead man to life (2Kings 13:20-21)
4. Jesus raised Jairus' daughter (Luke 8:51-55)
5. Jesus raised the son of a widow (Luke 7:11-15)
6. Jesus raised Lazarus after four days (John 11:41-42)

7. God the Father, God the Son, and God the Holy Spirit are all credited with raising Jesus from the dead (John 2:19; Galatians 1:1; Romans 8:11)
8. God the Father raised up numerous saints (Matthew 27:52)
9. Peter resurrected Tabitha/Dorcas (Acts 9:39-42)
10. Paul resurrected young Eutychus (Acts 20:9-10)

The only confirmed non-believer seemingly raised from the dead will be the Antichrist. Revelation 13:3 states, *"I saw one of his heads as if it had been slain, and his fatal wound was healed. And the whole earth was amazed and followed after the beast."*

In this chapter we saw Jesus, His apostles, and several other disciples having power and authority to heal anyone and everyone who came to them for a healing, and they healed any and every kind of illness, anytime, and every time, anywhere and everywhere they traveled. The only ones who did not receive a healing were those who did not come out for a healing.

In John 5 we see an interesting incongruity as Jesus selectively healed one out of many who were in need of healing at the pool of Bethesda. Some might ask "Where was His compassion?" Why select only one person when so many needed a touch of The Healer's hand.

The man who was healed had been ill for 38 years and unable to walk. He might have been one of those injured laborers who worked on Herod's Temple. Apparently, the man did not exhibit any faith in Jesus, so in all probability, the man wasn't even saved. Nor is it obvious in Scripture whether this man was any more righteous than the others surrounding the pool of Bethesda. Jesus probably used this man to provoke a response from the Jewish leaders since the healing occurred on a Sabbath day. Typical of Jesus' many other healings, He healed the man immediately and completely, and gave the man an unusual command not given to anyone else who came to Him – "Do not sin anymore, less something worse happens to you."

In essence, all ailments are due to sin since Adam's fall put the world under a curse of death. Some ailments are due to godly discipline, judgment, or, as in Job's case, for God's glory. Then there are sins which can cause specific illnesses to the bones, the heart, and the mind as noted in Psalms 38.

Scripture is clear that Jesus healed anyone and everyone of anything and everything. So, why did Jesus pick on just one lone individual to heal in this case and avoided showing compassion to the other sick people surrounding the pool of Bethesda? Consider this – Jesus healed ALL those who came to Him for healings, BUT He healed selectively those who did not seek Him out (e.g., raising the widow's son and the healings of various demoniacs).

Those at the pool of Bethesda did not seek out Jesus, but instead sought for a healing from a mythical or legendary source. Those who made it to the water after supposedly an angel stirred it received, at best, a psychosomatic healing.

Also, consider that Jesus' priority was on teaching, which provided permanent healing to the soul. Physical healings and miracles were secondary since they would only provide temporary comfort while on earth.

Chapter 3
Healings in the Book of Acts and the Epistles

And it happened that the father of Publius was lying in bed afflicted with recurrent fever and dysentery; and Paul went in to see him and after he had prayed, he laid his hands on him and healed him. After this had happened, the rest of the people on the island who had diseases were coming to him and getting cured. Acts 28:8-9

Apostolic Healings and Miracles

As we move into the book of Acts we see the same types of healings as we see in the Gospels. The apostles and certain other disciples healed anyone and everyone of anything and everything, any time and every time, anywhere and everywhere they went.

Throughout the book of Acts, Luke, the author, was meticulous with details. Classical scholar and historian, Colin Hemer, chronicled Luke's accuracy in the book of Acts with painstaking detail. Hemer identified 84 facts just in the last 16 chapters of Acts, which have been confirmed by historical and archeological records. Luke also records 35 miracles in Acts. What is interesting of Luke's account is that all miraculous incidences are without embellishment, lending additional credibility to each of them. If Luke was accurate with trivial details such as peculiar town names, the names of ships, and titles of officials for that time period, then it stands to reason he would also be just as meticulous in recording the miraculous accurately.

In Luke's Gospel and the Book of Acts he accurately identifies more than 100 historical names and places, including the water depth near a harbor. So, if he is accurate with his secular details, it stands to reason when he states that a miracle happened it has the same reliability. In fact, Luke records in Acts that Paul temporarily blinded a sorcerer (13:11), cured a man who was crippled from birth (14:8), exorcized an evil spirit from a possessed girl (16:18), performed many other miracles which convinced many Ephesians to renounce sorcery (19:11-20), healed Publius' father of dysentery, and also healed any and all others who were sick on the island of Malta (28:8-9).

Before expounding further on Paul's miraculous accomplishments, we cannot forget about the miracles Peter and some of the other disciples performed. Like the crowd incidences highlighted in the Gospels, Luke also records healings of similar multitudes in the Book of Acts.

Acts 5:12 depicts many signs and wonders taking place among the people by the hands of the apostles. Presumably, Matthias, who was selected to replace Judas by the casting of dice, was also able to work miraculous wonders right alongside the other apostles. In Acts 5:15 we see the crowds even carried their sick out into the streets and laid them on cots and pallets so when Peter came by at least his shadow might fall on them for a healing. Acts 5:16 records people from the cities near Jerusalem were coming together, bringing the sick or afflicted with unclean spirits, and, just as we saw in Matthew's Gospel, they were ALL healed.

How many can we predict to be in these gatherings? Hundreds? Thousands? More than ten thousand? Considering the fervor of the Jewish rulers to search out and apprehend these apostles to quell the potential for any uprising, multiple thousands would seem appropriate. This would be similar to the crowds of 4,000 and 5,000 we saw in Matthew. Plus Luke records 3,000 souls accepting the Gospel in Acts 3:41, and another 5,000 men in Acts 4:4.

Acts also records the miraculous wonders performed by several disciples, such as Stephen and Philip who were among the first set of deacons chosen by the early church of Jerusalem. Acts 6:8 states that Stephen, being full of grace and power, was performing great wonders and signs among the people; and Acts 8:5-7 records Philip going down to the city of Samaria and, there, the crowds heard and saw the signs he was performing. Unclean spirits were being cast out and those who had been paralyzed and lame were ALL healed.

Ananias, a disciple identified in Acts 9:10-17, gave Paul his sight after he lost it on the road to Damascus with his encounter with Jesus. Ananias, it is recorded, also gave Paul the Holy Spirit. That would make Ananias the only non-apostle who was given the ability to render the Holy Spirit to someone, in this case to a chosen Apostle of Jesus Christ.

Luke records in Acts 9:34-42 Peter healing Aeneas, who was paralyzed and bedridden for eight years. This miracle prompted many to believe in the Lord. Luke also records in the same chapter Peter raising Tabitha from the dead and, once again, many believed after hearing about this miraculous resurrection. It is interesting in this passage Luke records many believing and accepting Jesus as Lord as a result of these supernatural miracles. We saw similar incidences in the Gospels where the Lord's miracles prompted many to believe.

3. HEALINGS IN THE BOOK OF ACTS AND THE EPISTLES

The people of this first century era were not unaccustomed to healings and miracles. In fact, B. B. Warfield writes that "heretics [and the heathen] had miracles to appeal to... from time immortal."[9] So, what compelled many to accept the Gospel message as true over all other forms of healings and miracles they experienced or heard about? They realized the authenticity of the apostolic message from these valid signs and wonders. There was no trickery or scamming for money. The healings were rendered free of charge and they were complete, painless, and instantaneous.

Naturally, we would think, such wonders would entice people everywhere within a day's walking distance to bring their sick out to the healers, and that is exactly what we see in both the Gospels and Acts. In fact, so many sought out Jesus and His apostles that Mark 3:20 records that *"the crowd gathered to such an extent that they could not even eat a meal."*

Luke continues recording healing phenomena as Paul consumes the latter chapters of Acts. Paul and Barnabas, in Acts 14:3, spent a long time in Iconium speaking boldly, and the Lord granted that signs and wonders be done by their hands. Then we see in Acts 19:11-12 God performed extraordinary miracles by the hands of Paul, so that handkerchiefs or aprons were even carried from his body to the sick, and the diseases left them and evil spirits went out.

In our modern times TV preachers have offered similar healing artifacts for as low as a $9.95 donation. The truly sad

---

[9]Warfield, B. B. (Originally Published 1918, Republished 2012). *Counterfeit Miracles*. New York: Charles Scribner's Sons (1918) and Forgotten Books (2012), 43

part about this travesty is that people buy those things expecting a miraculous healing. Some would say a psychosomatic healing is better than no healing.

Paul eventually has a resurrection added to his credit. While preaching into the wee hours of the morning, a young man, possibly a teenager, by the name of Eutychus drifted off to sleep and fell out of a window he was perched in. Acts 20:9-10 records that Paul went down and fell upon the lad, and was picked up dead. After embracing him, Paul said, *"Do not be troubled, for his life is in him."* Was this a valid resurrection from the dead or did Eutychus just have the wind knocked out of him? We can give Paul credit here for a resurrection since Luke, who, as we have shown to be an acclaimed historian, recorded that the lad was picked up dead and not simply unconscious.

Healings and Miracles in the Epistles. When we leave the Gospels and the book of Acts and traverse through the Epistles, we immediately see that something has changed in regards to healings and miracles. The change is so drastic it begs the question whether or not God is still working supernatural healings and miracles following the end of the apostolic era. In fact, it looks like supernatural healings and miracles ceased even before the apostles had all died.

In brief, there are five unique incidences often mentioned to give credence to God changing His ways with the miraculous. Each of these incidences reveal an Apostle who once was able to heal anyone and everyone of anything and everything, and even raise the dead, to now being unable to heal faithful disciples of whatever was ailing them.

3. Healings in the Book of Acts and the Epistles

Paul's Thorn in the Flesh. The first incident is found in 2Corinthians 12:1-10. This is the passage where Paul made it clear that God would not heal him of his "thorn in the flesh" even though Paul prayed three times for relief. This thorn was to keep Paul humbled after he experienced a heavenly vision. This incident of him receiving a heavily vision to motivate godly service is not normative for anyone else in the church.

Many theologians suspect the thorn had something to do with either bad eye sight or a facial disfigurement. This is possibly gleaned from a brutal stoning recorded in Acts 14:19 where Paul was stoned and *"dragged out of the city, supposing him to be dead."* Paul could have easily suffered a broken eye socket or two, a fractured nose, broken cheekbones, broken or lost teeth, and a cracked skull. If Paul suffered a severe concussion from this stoning, lingering physical issues, such as stroke-like symptoms, could last the rest of his life if God didn't miraculously heal him.

Another interesting aspect of this thorn in the flesh is that it is also called a "messenger of Satan" with the sole purpose of tormenting Paul. It seems odd that Satan would do something to Paul to help him stay humbled and more useful for God's service. So this "messenger of Satan" may just be a colloquial phrase used in conjunction with "thorn in the flesh" to clearly indicate a physical handicap of some sort and, possibly, not a literal demonic influence. Since we live in a fallen word it is not uncommon, though, to label all misfortunes as being somehow from Satan.

Whether Paul's thorn in the flesh was due to direct demonic influence or due to a physical disfigurement another question we need to ask is "do we have a contradiction in

Scripture?" Jesus gave numerous commands to His apostles and disciples regarding praying and receiving positive answers. These include: *"whatsoever you ask in prayer, believing, you shall receive"*; and *"if you say to this mountain, 'Be taken up and cast into the sea,' it will happen."* So, why didn't Paul get this thorn in his flesh removed when he asked in unwavering faith?

We can only take Paul at his word that his thorn in the flesh was a direct intervention by God to keep him humbled and useful after receiving a one-of-a-kind heavenly experience meant to motivate and focus his service at the highest level during intense persecution. Recall that five times Paul received thirty-nine lashings, three times he was beaten, once he was stoned, three times he was shipwrecked, and he spent a night and a day treading water (2Corinthians 11:24-25).

His thorn in the flesh and his inability to get it removed through natural or supernatural means was, in essence, unique to his situation and we cannot extrapolate it and use it to justify why supernatural miracles have ceased for our day and age. It would be poor hermeneutics. We have to move on to other incidences in Scripture.

Epaphroditus – Sick to the Point of Death. The second incident where an apostle was not able to render an instantaneous and spontaneous healing is found in Philippians 2:25-30. This is where Paul stated he was at God's mercy for Him to restore Epaphroditus from a near death illness. Epaphroditus, if you recall *"was sick to the point of death, but God had mercy on him, and not on him only but also on [Paul], so that [Paul] would not have sorrow upon sorrow."*

The sickness seemed to have been a prolonged illness that went from bad to worse. This is gleaned from the Philippians first hearing about Epaphroditus being sick. Then, after some time had elapsed, Paul heard about the concern of the Philippians and stated that God eventually had mercy on the situation and allowed Epaphroditus to recover from his severe illness.

I can picture Epaphroditus being sick with something similar to influenza. Since Paul was devoted to praying, it seems reasonable he would have prayed for Epaphroditus upon the initial onset of mild flu-like symptoms. After all, Epaphroditus was a servant of God on a mission from God to bring relief to one of the Lord's eminent apostles. Paul even called Epaphroditus a "messenger" of the Philippians. The Greek word used here for "messenger" <apostolos> is often translated "apostle." So, in effect, Epaphroditus was a highly regarded man of God within the Philippian church and highly esteemed by the Apostle Paul. Wasn't Epaphroditus, therefore, worthy of a healing before his illness turned from being uncomfortable to being deadly? Why did God wait so long?

We even see in Paul's closing remarks to the Philippians that he was not alone in this struggle. Even though Paul was probably in a Roman prison cell when he wrote this letter, Philippians 4:21-22 states, *"The brethren who are with me greet you. All the saints greet you, especially those of Caesar's household."* These dear saints, who were probably discipled by Paul, in all probability knew of Epaphroditus' dire condition and assuredly prayed for him as well during his illness. Epaphroditus was possibly staying at a church member's house while he ministered to Paul in prison. He might have even contracted his illness as a result of one of his trips to Paul's prison. Sanitary conditions would have been atrocious with open sewage and impure drinking water.

Why didn't God heal Epaphroditus earlier when the Christians gathered together for prayer as they were accustomed? Scripture encourages us to pray for all men. Matthew 18:19 states, *"that if two of you agree on earth about anything that they may ask, it shall be done for them by My Father who is in heaven."* Again, do we have a contradiction in Scripture or can we come to grips that God has changed His ways with ceasing to render instantaneous and spontaneous supernatural healings and miracles?

Let's back up to the question of "why did God wait so long" to heal Epaphroditus. A possible answer to that question is found in Isaiah 41. There, we see a picture of God's people thirsting for water to the point of death. God did not rescue them when they were just a little thirsty, but waited till they were parched and their tongues were basically cleaving to the roof of their mouths. The answer God gave clearly conveyed that neither their own abilities, nor fate, nor coincidence, nor were other gods involved in answering their prayers or getting them out of their dilemma. It was undeniably God who rescued them.

3. HEALINGS IN THE BOOK OF ACTS AND THE EPISTLES

✦

The afflicted and needy are seeking water, but there is none, and their tongue is parched with thirst; I, the LORD, will answer them Myself, As the God of Israel I will not forsake them. ...That they may see and recognize, and consider and gain insight as well, that the hand of the LORD has done this, and the Holy One of Israel has created it. Isaiah 41:17, 20

✦

Timothy's Frequent Infirmities. The third incidence where an Apostle seemingly lost the ability to work instantaneous and spontaneous supernatural healings and miracles, again, involves Paul. In 1Timothy 5:23 we find that Paul could not heal Timothy, but told him instead, to take some wine (in effect, medicine) for his frequent infirmities.

✦

Drink no longer water, but use a little wine for thy stomach's sake and thine often infirmities. 1Timothy 5:23

✦

Where was Paul's handkerchief that once healed multitudes? Why didn't Paul tell Timothy to seek out someone with the gift of healings or of miracles or of faith? Why couldn't Paul heal Timothy remotely as Jesus sometimes did with a few people? Why couldn't Paul, Timothy, and other saints just simply pray when two or more had gathered together to receive from the Lord what they asked for?

Timothy, like Epaphroditus, was an exceptional servant of God. Unlike many of us, who have not yet shed any of our blood in the service of the Gospel, Timothy had no qualms about getting circumcised to be able to win more Jews to the Lord – and he was a half-breed, his mother being a Jewess and his dad a Greek (Acts 16:1-3). What sacrificial 'agape' love Timothy had for God's people the Jews, for Paul, and for the Church.

We are told in 1Timothy 5:23 that he suffered from stomach problems and from other *"often infirmities."* Paul once healed a man of dysentery and subsequently healed everyone who was sick on the island of Malta. Surely Timothy's ailments were very much in line with what Paul had healed in times past. Why did Timothy have to take medicine (wine) for his illnesses? Did someone lose their faith, or was sin somehow involved, or did God change His ways?

We can only come to one of three conclusions. Either we have contradictions in Scripture; or Paul and/or Timothy had sin in their lives, to include a lack of faith; or God changed the rules of the game. We will address contradictions in Scripture in more detail later in this chapter, but suffice it to say that contradictions within Scripture are not a viable conclusion since Scripture is not contradictory to itself. The issue would be more of our erroneous understanding of Scripture.

Also, if Paul and/or Timothy had sin in their lives even that would not factor in as to why Timothy didn't receive a healing, because Jesus had no problems healing sinners. Jesus even healed people who had weak faith or no faith at all. Even Judas, the son of perdition, apparently had power from on High to heal people supernaturally.

Paul and Timothy were very mature believers, who continually grew in their faith as the years passed, and grew closer to the Lord on a daily basis. They would also have been keenly aware of God's will for their lives. And, they would definitely be sensitive to any sin in their lives which would need to be confessed and dealt with, if there was any. Sin, therefore, is not a viable consideration why Timothy could not receive a supernatural healing.

We are left with only one viable conclusion in this matter. God had altered his approach to working supernatural healings and miracles, and this approach changed even before the apostles had all died off. But we are not finished looking at all the evidence yet.

Trophimus – Left Sick in Miletus. We get to the fourth incident where Paul the Apostle, once more, is unable to heal another servant of God. In 2Timothy 4:20 we find that Paul could not heal Trophimus, but had to leave him sick in Miletus.

Erastus remained at Corinth, but Trophimus I left sick at Miletus.
2Timothy 4:20

We are once again left with an unanswered question of why this was so. Was Trophimus' illness too hard for God to heal? Since nothing is too hard for God (Jeremiah 32:27), we can scratch that question off from our list as being viable. And no sin is obvious in the passage. As noted previously, sin would not prevent a healing if the Holy Spirit was truly working supernaturally at this time.

Trophimus' illness must also have been a prolonged illness since Paul gave up waiting for him to get well so that he could keep to his traveling itinerary. When Paul said that he had to leave him since he was too sick to travel with him we can logically assume Paul either left Trophimus in good hands with other caretakers or that Trophimus was not in a near death illness as Epaphroditus was.

Call for the Elders. Finally, we get to the fifth incidence in Scripture where it looks like God drastically changed His approach to working instantaneous and spontaneous healings and miracles. In James 5:16 the sick are instructed to call for the elders, to confess their sins to one another, and to pray for one another so they may be healed.

⌘

Is anyone among you sick? Then he must call for the elders of the church and they are to pray over him, anointing him with oil in the name of the Lord; and the prayer offered in faith will restore the one who is sick, and the Lord will raise him up, and if he has committed sins, they will be forgiven him. Therefore, confess your sins to one another, and pray for one another so that you may be healed. The effective prayer of a righteous man can accomplish much.
James 5:14-16

⌘

There is no indication for the sick to call for the ones with spiritual gifts for them to receive instantaneous restoration of their health. Is this a new order for the church to follow or is it in addition to being able to call for those with the ability to heal? When we consider the whole counsel of God, this passage seems to be a new church process to implement for healings in lieu of calling for anyone with the gift or gifts to heal.

Why call for the elders of the church? Why not call for the deacons who had the responsibility to look after weaker members of the fellowship, or to call for those with gifts of helps within the church? After all, the elders would be busy with praying and teaching God's word. Who, however, is better to assess a needful situation within the church than spiritually mature elders? They thoroughly know God's word, God's will, and possibly each member of their church?

The elders may not be medical doctors, but they would know the Bible well enough to assess if sin is playing a role with a person's physical, mental, social, and spiritual health. This is where spiritual maturity and wise discernment pays dividends. Since every needy case is different, it takes the wisdom of mature pastors, elders, or other biblically astute church members to assess the root problem and figure out how best to respond – even how fast to respond. There is no precise answer to the many scenarios which could come before a church elder.

Elders have to factor the various details of each situation, including such things as prodigal behavior before rendering a prognosis. From a scriptural perspective, the main requirement for elders is to have solid knowledge of the Bible and good access to the Throne of Grace to properly assess and address the needs of the needy and hopefully get them back on their feet in quick fashion. Hence, all the more reason for mature spiritual leaders to be called for, since they have a stronger tendency to depend on God's specific directions and principles found in His Word. This often includes questioning, investigating, assessing, validating, praying about and discerning the needs that come before them.

What does sin have to do with someone's health? Scripture actually has a lot to say about the connections between sin and one's physical, mental, social, and spiritual wellbeing. Consider these few passages from Psalms and Proverbs.

Psalms 31:10 *My strength has failed because of my iniquity, and my body has wasted away.*

Psalms 38:3 *There is no soundness in my flesh because of Your indignation; there is no health in my bones because of my sin.*

Proverbs 3:7-8 *Fear the LORD and turn away from evil. It will be healing to your body and refreshment to your bones.*

Proverbs 4:22 *For [the words of God] are life to those who find them and health to all their body.*

Proverbs 13:12 *Hope deferred makes the heart sick.*

Proverbs 14:30 *A tranquil heart is life to the body, but passion is rottenness to the bones.*

Proverbs 16:24 *Pleasant words are as honeycomb, sweet to the soul, and health to the bones.*

Proverbs 17:22 *A joyful heart is good medicine, but a broken spirit dries up the bones.*

Proverbs 18:14 *The spirit of a man can endure his sickness, but as for a broken spirit who can bear it?*

Medical science supports the concepts that encouraging words, supportive family, and hope for the future help with the healing process for ailments faster than if a patient contends with despair and criticism from self and close friends and family. Medical science also shows that unbiblical behavior such as lying, cheating, stealing, adultery, and other immoral acts put undue stress on the body and mind, often rendering stress-related illnesses such as high blood pressure to physical ailments such as sexually-transmitted diseases.

Godly Intervention Through Prayers and Anointings. According to James, the elders provide two beneficial elements to the sick for their expedited healing – prayers and anointing. Scripture, especially the New Testament, talks about praying prolifically throughout its pages. We are instructed how to pray, where to pray, when to pray, how often to pray, what and whom to pray for, whom to pray to, and why to pray.

We are to be devoted to prayer, we are to pray unceasingly, we are to pray for all men and women, and the effectual prayers of a righteous person accomplishes much. All these specifics on praying convey that God has chosen to intervene into the affairs of the world through our prayers. History can be changed, men and women can be saved and be saved sooner, be healed, be protected, and we can be used for God to accomplish His will – all through the prayers of men and women, boys and girls.

In comparison, the anointing process is seldom addressed. We only have a few passages in the New Testament, such as Mark 6:13 and James 5:14, which simply state that anointing of oil was performed. In all probability, the healings could have easily been accomplished with the same results even if the anointing of oil was not administered.

What, then, is the purpose of anointing someone with oil? We don't even know the actual ingredients of the oil used, the ratios of any blended elements, and the incubating time to cure the mixture to make it the most beneficial as a medicinal salve. More than likely it was olive oil, but was it virgin olive oil, extra virgin olive oil, light olive oil, or was it mixed with other ingredients to somehow render the optimum healing affect?

Also, was the oil applied as a medicinal anti-bacterial salve, or was it drunk in small doses or large doses, or was it symbolic of God being involved in the healing process, or did it provide some kind of psychosomatic affect? Was it splashed on, sprinkled on, poured on, or did it matter how it was applied? We just do not really know and must speculate the reasons for its use.

There is a hermeneutic principle which basically states that when Scripture gives limited information on a topic, usually it is only intended for the original audience. Future readers can derive principles, but not specific or dogmatic doctrines from it. From a biblical perspective we can admit that the oil possessed no inherent magical properties often ascribed by those who believe in relic worship. Relic worship will be addressed in the next chapter.

In the Old Testament, prophets, priests, and kings were anointed with oil or blood in a commensuration service to officially recognize and commission them for the service they were designated to do. The oil is seen as symbolic to receiving God's acknowledgement and blessings to proceed in their functionary roles with His continued oversight.

Anointing with blood was symbolic of substitutionary atonement or for cleansing reasons. A peculiar practice of anointing in the Old Testament is when the right earlobe, the right thumb, and right big toe were anointed by the priest.

The true meaning of this practice seems to be forever lost in history of its actual significance. We can only speculate.

There was only one type of individual who had their earlobes, thumbs and big toes anointed with oil in this manner – a cleansed leper. Now, the Levitical priests had their right earlobes, right thumbs, and right big toes anointed, but their appendages were anointed with the blood of a sacrificial animal and not with oil (Leviticus 8). A leper who was cured had his right appendages anointed both with blood and with oil as noted in Leviticus 14.

Here is John Gill's (1697-1771) commentary on Leviticus 14:17: The right earlobe, the right thumb, and the right big toe "signify that these parts in the leprous sinner need to be sanctified by the grace of the Spirit of God, comparable to oil, with which all the Lord's people are anointed, and is that unction they receive from the Holy One, their great High Priest; by this the ear is sanctified so as to hear the word, so as to understand it and mix it with faith; and the thumb of the right hand having oil put on that, **may signify** that the actions of good men are influenced by the Spirit of God, who works in them both to will and to do, and without whose grace they can do nothing in a spiritual manner; and the great toe of the right foot, the instrument of walking, being anointed with the same, **may denote** that it is through the grace of God saints have their conversation in the world in simplicity and godly sincerity, and as becomes the Gospel of Christ: the oil was to be put."

Notice that this great expositor used the term "may signify" and "may denote" to the meaning of this ritual. Again, we just do not know with certainty the full significance for anointing with oil, though we can dogmatically say there are no magical properties to the application of oil. What we can say is that the anointing process was purely symbolic in nature as a testimony to others of God's acknowledgement and involvement in the healing process.

In Matthew 8:4, when Jesus healed a leper, He commanded him to *"tell no one; but go, show yourself to the priest and present the offering that Moses commanded, as a testimony to them."* This would have been the only recorded incident of a leper being cured in the Bible and undergoing the ritual described in Leviticus 14. This testimony to the priests is so significant from God's perspective that this healing is also recorded in Mark 1:44 and in Luke 5:14. But why the command not to tell anyone, and to keep it low key? Surely, the priests would have asked the man how he was cured. Possibly, Jesus tried to limit the publicity of His healing campaign for a bit longer.

Pentecostals seem prone to view many objects of their faith as having healing properties. It could be the purchasing of an "anointed" piece of cloth, or wrapping themselves in a prayer shawl, or hearing a shofar being played, or even getting anointed with olive oil, which could bring the healing they so eagerly desire. There are even claims of such healings, but they are always on the order of the psychosomatic or functional disorders.

Godly Intervention Through Sovereign Control. Besides intervening through our prayers God also intervenes into the affairs of man through direct and indirect means. Some believe God just set the universe in motion and He just sits back and watches events play out as He sovereignly designed them to. A more biblical approach is that God actively participates in the affairs of men on a daily basis, and He desires to do so much more if only His people would pray more.

God, however, is so sovereign He is fully capable of accomplishing His will in all areas and in all generations whether or not men and women pray as they should. He knows the end from the beginning, and He knows the beginning from the end. He has sovereign control over the weather, over nature, over time, over national economies, over all satanic activities, and over each and every individual without turning anyone into a robot. What a great God we serve.

WHAT CHANGED BETWEEN ACTS AND THE EPISTLES

Again, what changed between what we see in Acts and the Epistles in regards to the cessation of supernatural signs and wonders, healings and miracles? In the book of Acts, the apostles and disciples were noted to heal anyone and everyone of anything and everything, any time and every time, anywhere and everywhere they went. But in the Epistles we see that Paul could not heal Epaphroditus, Timothy, nor Trophimus of their ailments, much less get himself healed of his own thorn in the flesh. And we find James telling believers to call for the elders and to confess their sins to receive physical healings.

If we look at the timeline of when Acts and the Epistles were written, we can see the chronology of events line up where the supernatural healings and miracles seemed to have stopped after Acts was written (60s A.D.) and definitely before Revelation was penned in the early 90s A.D. It looks from Scripture we will not see supernatural healings and miracles until we see the two witnesses identified in Revelation 11 come onto the world scene.

What changed after Acts? After all, if God truly changed something as fundamental as working supernatural wonders, which were used to confirm the deity of Christ and propel the early church into existence and onto a sound footing, it seems reasonable for God to provide ample evidence of such a cessation in His word. And that is exactly what we do find.

Beginning with Romans and continuing through Hebrews, we see Paul and the writer of Hebrews addressing signs and wonders either in past or aorist tense, and even perfect tense, but rarely in present or future tenses. The rare exceptions noted in 1Corinthians and Galatians will show that the supernatural wonders were possibly still active at the time those two epistles were written, but it is not an absolute.

It should be noted, however, Paul accused the Corinthians of being infants in Christ, and he called the Galatians foolish. So, even if a church has all the gifts and they can work miracles extraordinaire, that is no guarantee they will be mature believers or have doctrinal purity. In addition, as we noted in Matthew 7, working signs and wonders doesn't even guarantee one's salvation.

Paul states in Romans 15:19, "*...in the power of signs and wonders, in the power of the Spirit; so that from Jerusalem and round about as far as Illyricum I* ***have fully preached*** *the gospel of Christ.*" He spoke this using what is called the perfect tense, which indicates an action that was completed and need not be repeated. In essence, Paul said 'I preached the Gospel in times past using supernatural signs and wonders, and that is all that was needed to get things going.'

The continual need to preach the Gospel in the power of the Holy Spirit is not in question since there are numerous other Scriptures which explicitly teach the need for the power of the Holy Spirit as a requirement to effectively preach the Gospel. Just a few verses before verse 19 Paul declares the following, *"Now may the God of hope fill you with all joy and peace in believing [the Gospel], so that you will abound in hope by the power of the Holy Spirit"* (Romans 15:13). Abounding in hope does not allude to signs and wonders, but to the more permanent fixation of better things to come from an eternal perspective.

Those of the Pentecostal persuasion often equate the "power of the Holy Spirit" to always include signs and wonders, but that is bad hermeneutics. The true power of the Holy Spirit is not in temporal healings and miracles which barely last until the next disease comes along, but in the permanent transformation of an unsaved Hell-bound individual into a saved Heaven-bound saint, and the transformation of an immature believer into one that mirrors the perfect image of Christ.

In 1Corinthians 2:4-5, Paul states the following *"...my message and my preaching **were** not in persuasive words of wisdom, but in demonstration of the Spirit and of power so that your faith would not rest on the wisdom of men, but on the power of God."* This passage is implied to be in past tense. Why didn't Paul say he was still preaching or will continue to preach in the demonstration and power of the Holy Spirit with signs and wonders?

The only conclusion we can draw is that something had changed by this time. Whether supernatural signs and wonders were still able to be worked or not did not matter. Paul no longer needed to preach in the demonstration of the Holy Spirit with signs and wonders to be effective. Our faith can still rest on the power of God with His ability to permanently transform lives without working supernaturally. The power of God is now revealed through providential healings and miracles and not in supernatural healings and miracles.

One of the more controversial passages used by cessationists to prove their viewpoint is 1Corinthians 13:10, *"But when the perfect* [complete] *comes, the partial* [the gifts] *will be done away with."* This seems to be a weak passage as a proof text for the cessation of the gifts since Paul was not specific with what he meant by "perfect." There is just nothing there to grab hold of and be absolute about. We can only speculate what the "perfect" or "complete" element might be. It could be the closure of the New Testament, or it could be the coming of Christ, or it could be a host of other things.

Paul is only laying out a general principle in this passage that immature practices cease when a mature artifact has made its appearance. In the case of some of the gifts ceasing Paul does not stipulate when, and he probably did not know himself when or if they would cease at this time.

John MacArthur records that F. F. Bruce suggests that the *"perfect"* is love itself; B. B. Warfield contends it is the completed canon of Scripture (cf. James 1:25); Robert Thomas argues it is the mature church (cf. Ephesians 4:11-13); Richard Gaffin asserts it is the return of Christ; and Thomas Edgar concludes it is the individual believer's entrance into heavenly glory (cf. 2Corinthians 5:8). Though these scholars disagree on the identification of the "perfect," they all reach the same conclusion – namely, that the miraculous and revelatory gifts have ceased.[10]

1Corinthians 13:12 states, *"For now we see in a mirror dimly, but then face to face; now I know in part, but then I will know fully."* This passage adds a unique consideration to what the "*perfect*" or "*complete*" element might be. It is possible Paul is alluding to the time of his death as the demarcation for the cessation of the supernatural gifts. This, too, however, is more speculation than an absolute rendering. What we can walk away with in this passage is "love" is key to resolving any and all conflicts within the church and within the home.

After all, chapters 12 through 14 are actually one paragraph in the Greek that Paul constructed to address and resolve a particular problem in the Corinthian church. Agape love was the crucial ingredient needed to honestly work through all the issues they had. Faith and hope are the other two ingredients, but they have their shortcomings. If you think about it, when we get to Heaven, we won't need faith any longer because we will have facts to deal with, and we will not need hope since our hope will be realized, but we will always have love.

---

[10] John MacArthur, *Strange Fire,* Nelson Books (Nashville, TN 2013), 148

A stronger passage to use to prove the cessation of the gifts is 2Corinthians 12:12 where Paul states that *"Truly the signs of an apostle* ***were worked*** *among you in all patience, in signs, and wonders, and mighty deeds."* The signs, wonders and mighty deeds of an apostle were worked in the past. The tense is aorist, which is characterized by its emphasis on punctiliar action; that is, the concept of the verb is considered without regard for past, present, or future time. There is no direct or clear English equivalent for this tense, though it is generally rendered as a simple past tense in most translations. What is interesting to note is that Paul did not convey that apostolic signs were presently being worked or will be continuously worked, but had been worked previously in sufficient detail to accomplish what God intended.

One of the unique apostolic signs was the granting of the Holy Spirit to various people groups. Philip, even though he performed numerous healings and miracles, could not give the Holy Spirit to the Samaritans. Peter had to be present for that event (Acts 8). Also, when Cornelius and his family received the Holy Spirit as recorded in Acts 10, Peter had to be present. A search party was even sent out for him.

Paul gave the Holy Spirit to the Ephesian believers in Acts 19. Since we can only prove things according to Scripture, we have to assume the Holy Spirit can only be given by no one else other than an Apostle of Jesus Christ.

Other unique signs of an Apostle involved how God used specific objects such as Peter's shadow and Paul's handkerchief as instruments of healing, but these seem to be unique one-of-a-kind occurrences. The book of Acts fails to support the continuationist view since no consistent pattern is evident. We can only prove what is true from the proper interpretation of Scripture, and not from anyone's experiences.

Another passage for cessationists is Hebrews 2:3-4 where the author states the Gospel "***was confirmed*** *[aorist tense] unto us by THEM that heard Him; God also* ***testifying*** *[present tense] both by signs and wonders and by various miracles and by gifts of the Holy Spirit according to His own will.*" Who were "them that heard him"? Those would be the apostles and early disciples such as Stephen, Ananias, Philip, and Barnabas.

Some continuationists might argue that the usage of present tense in "*God also* ***testifying*** *[present tense] both by signs and wonders*" nullifies the previous use of the aorist tense, but that is not based on sound hermeneutics. In essence, the author of Hebrews is saying that God confirmed [past tense] the Gospel by using [present tense] signs and wonders. An example would be that President Kennedy was killed [past tense] by an assassin using {present tense] a high powered rifle. The action is complete without further use of the elements involved.

The Supernatural in the Epistles. There are only three incidences in the Epistles where it could be construed that supernatural activities were active, and thereby, possibly continuous throughout church history. These incidences are found in 1Corinthians, Galatians, and 1Thessalonians.

In 1Corinthians 14:39 Paul commands the believers to "*desire earnestly to prophesy, and do not forbid to speak in tongues.*" Cessationists have to acknowledge, based on this passage, that when 1Corinthians was written the gifts were possibly still active at that time (~55 AD), so it was appropriate for Paul to make such a command. If this passage was truly meant to be continuous throughout church history, then just the continuance of prophesies would justify the continued growth of Scripture beyond the current 66 books of the Bible we now have, and have had since the earliest testimonies of the early Christian Fathers and finally acknowledged and ratified as early as the Council of Carthage in 397 A.D.

Continuationists have to acknowledge, and they have, that prophecies today are not the same as found in Scripture, which means for us to desire to prophecy and not to forbid the speaking of tongues is not applicable today even by continuationists' standards. Therefore, it is imperative and incumbent upon astute church leaders to stop the practice of any spiritual counterfeits, and properly instruct their congregants on what true spiritual gifts and fruit are.

The next passage, which alludes to supernatural miracles being active, is Galatians 3:5. This passage states that Jesus, "*who provides you with the Spirit and works miracles among you, [does He] do it by the works of the Law, or by hearing with faith?*" Galatians was written early (possibly between 51-53 AD), so supernatural miracles and wonders were probably still active at this time, but the text does not preclude miracles being worked only by "those who heard Him"

Continuationist, Robert L. Saucy, in his contribution to Wayne Grudem's book, *Are Miraculous Gifts for Today,* had this to say about Galatians 3:5: "This passage is best understood as parallel to Hebrews 2:3-4. The entire section [Galatians 3:1-5] focuses on the initial reception of the Spirit by the Galatian believers. Paul's joining of the giving of the Spirit with the working of miracles, therefore, suggests that these miracles among the Galatians were closely connected with their initial reception of the Spirit, which in turn accompanied the initial proclamation of the Gospel by the apostle (and perhaps others with him). Thus the text, while not limiting miracles to the apostles or others who proclaimed the Gospel, does associate the miraculous activity to this ministry of the first witnesses. This passage does not necessarily mean that miracles happened only at the very first preaching, but possibly suggests that the miraculous activity may well have continued among believers in Galatia, similar to the miracle-producing gifts in the church at Corinth as depicted in 1Corinthians 12:10, although how long the activity continued is not specified."[11]

Longenecker's commentary on this matter states that the question of the continuance of miracles is not entirely clear in the language of the verse. While most interpreters see the present tense of the participles as indicating some continuity in both participles, i.e., in the supplying of the Spirit and working of miracles, the verbs of the sentence are unexpressed and therefore have to be supplied from the text.[12]

Burton adds that the choice of the present tense rather than the aorist shows that the apostle has in mind an

---

[11]Wayne G. Grudem, general editor. (1996). *Are Miraculous Gifts for Today*. Grand Rapids: Zondervan, 110

[12] Longenecker, Galatians, 99, 105

experience extended enough to be thought of as in progress, but not that it is in progress at the time of writing.[13]

A little more detail was warranted on this passage (Galatians 3:5) to show the thought processes of several commentators of differing persuasions. Saucy is not a cessationist, yet he sides with cessationists that this passage, along with Hebrews 2:3-4, does not convey the continuance of supernatural gifts throughout church history.

In 1Thessalonians 5:20-21, Paul tells the believers not to despise prophecies, but to prove everything. We probably need to assume that "prophecies" were delivered as a result of someone either having the gift of prophecy, or they were a designated prophet, such as Agabus, or one of the prophesying daughters of Philip. This letter was also written very early (~51 AD), so we can assume the gifts of the Holy Spirit were active at this time.

Even Paul acknowledged in 2Corinthians 10:10 that people rejected his preaching (*"his speech is contemptible"*) and possibly his prophetic utterances. We also have to realize when God truly spoke through a prophet, to despise the prophecy was to show contempt for God and for His word. So this was a very serious warning. The despising of a prophecy, however, was the despising of a valid revelation from God, not the despising of false prophecies.

Again, we are faced with a dire issue. If prophets and prophecies are still active today, then we should see the word of God growing beyond the current 66 books. All

[13] Burton, Commentary on Galatians, 152

Christendom, however, acknowledges the closure of canon. Based on that, we also have to acknowledge the cessation of prophecies. We cannot have a closed canon and still accommodate prophetic utterances, whether they are by the gift of prophecy, tongues, interpretation of tongues, or by the word of wisdom or knowledge.

Pentecostals, however, argue that prophecies declared by those with the gift of prophecy are different than biblical prophecies, with some prophecies allowing for errors. If that is true, then there is no way for anyone to be able to prove anything as valid or true. By default, then, we have to acknowledge that the office of prophets and the gift of prophecy have ceased. Else we have a door open for heresy to come boldly into the church – and that is exactly what has been and is happening within the Pentecostal movements.

Though the gifts of the Holy Spirit and the working of supernatural healings and miracles were possibly still prevalent at the time 1Corinthians and Galatians were written, both the Corinthians and the Galatians were the most immature group of believers Paul had to contend with. Therefore, being able to work miracles and having all the gifts of the Holy Spirit (the Corinthians came behind no gift as noted in 1Corinthians 1:7), does not provide or promote spiritual maturity or guarantee doctrinal purity or even one's salvation.

In 1Corinthians 3:1-3 Paul stated, *"I could not speak to you as to spiritual men, but as to men of flesh, as to infants in Christ. I gave you milk to drink, not solid food; for you were not yet able to receive it. Indeed, even now you are not yet able, for you are still fleshly. For since there is jealousy and strife among you."* In

Galatians 3:1-3 Paul lambasted those believers for succumbing so easily to legalistic practices and moving away from the truth of the Gospel message – *"you foolish Galatians, who has bewitched you…Are you so foolish? Having begun by the Spirit, are you now being perfected by the flesh?"*

Healings and Miracles in Revelation –A Change Up. The Revelation of Jesus Christ is awash with miraculous activities, especially as we enter Chapter 11 where we find the two witnesses performing supernatural wonders by instantaneously controlling weather phenomena and other events.

⌘

And if anyone wants to harm [My 2 witnesses], fire flows out of their mouth and devours their enemies; so if anyone wants to harm them, he must be killed in this way. These have the power to shut up the sky, so that rain will not fall during the days of their prophesying; and they have power over the waters to turn them into blood, and to strike the earth with every plague, as often as they desire. Revelation 11:5-6

⌘

Even Satan gets in the act as we see in Revelation 13 where the Antichrist is seemingly raised from being dead. He is the only non-believer to be resurrected. The purpose of raising the Antichrist by healing his fatal head wound is to achieve world dominion – *"…and the whole earth was amazed and followed after the beast"* (verse 4). Even the False Prophet is able to perform great signs, so that he even makes fire come down out of heaven to the earth (verses 13-14). The sole intent for these satanic wonders is to deceive those who dwell on the earth and to eventually get them to gather for the war of the great day of God, the Almighty (Revelation 16:14).

If supernatural healings and miracles were to be continuous throughout the church age, then when John penned Revelation 11 and described the miraculous wonders of the two witnesses they would not be notable since anybody with the gift of faith or miracles could easily work such wonders at will. The wonders to be performed by these two special witnesses include the ability to kill by fire (possibly lightening), to cause drought, able to turn water into blood, and to strike the earth with every conceivable plague as often as they desire.

Since the early Church was expected to grow exponentially as a mustard seed, supernatural miracles, if they were to be continuous down through the ages, would be very numerous and rather normal to expect. Such volume of miracles by the exponentially growing number of Christians would virtually dwarf the impact of these two witnesses in Revelation 11, who would only be around for 1,260 days, or about three and a half years. This argument alone nullifies the continuance of supernatural miracles throughout the Church age since the miracles of the two witnesses are given so much prominence in Revelation 11.

DO WE HAVE CONTRADICTIONS?

How do we handle apparent contradictions we find in Scripture? For example, as we see in John 14:13-14 below and in similar passages throughout the gospels we have tremendous promises from Jesus where we can get virtually every prayer answered. Yet, we saw in several epistles where an eminent apostle of Jesus Christ could not even cure other hard-working Christian servants of their ailments. Nor could the apostle cure himself of his own affliction. What gives? Do we have contradictions, or are there other mitigating factors we need to consider?

Whatever you ask in My name, that will I do, so that the Father may be glorified in the Son. If you ask Me anything in My name, I will do it. John 14:13-14

The Bare BONES of Biblical Principles. There is a wonderful acrostic to recall the basic biblical principles. BONES equates to the Balancing, Overriding, Negating, Explanatory, and Sequential principles often found in Scripture.

Balancing Principle. For example, a key balancing principle is Ephesians 4:15, which tells us to speak the truth in love. They both go hand in hand. If we were to speak the truth without love it would be tyranny, and if we were to love without having the truth we would be promoting licentiousness (or the license to do anything).

Overriding Principle. An overriding principle can be seen in 1Peter 2:13 where we are commanded to submit ourselves to every ordinance of man for the Lord's sake, yet this command would be overridden (as seen in Acts 4:19) if man's ordinance conflicted with God's ordinance. God's laws override man's laws.

Negating Principle. We are encouraged to give to the poor as highlighted in Matthew 19:21, but if the poor are lazy and slothful, we have to implement some tough love. If they don't work, they don't eat (1Thessalonians 3:10).

Explanatory Principle. A good example of an explanatory principle is found in Mark 2:27, where we see Jesus explaining why it was sometimes necessary and proper to work on the Sabbath, because "The Sabbath was made for man, and not man for the Sabbath."

Sequential Principle. 1John 1:9 is a good passage for a sequential principle. As the name indicates, a sequence of events needs to occur. In this case we need to confess and repent from any sin before we can be cleansed and restored to fellowship.

Perspective Principle. There is one more principle we need to look at and that is the perspective principle. This is where a passage either has an earthly perspective or a heavenly perspective. This principle, more than any other, helps to properly discern why Pentecostals err in their hermeneutics approach to Scripture. Since Pentecostals have a materialistic perspective they prefer to see passages of Scripture from an earthly perspective rather than from a heavenly perspective. For example, they are keen to highlight the "seed of faith" practice – sow now, reap now; give a lot, receive a lot; and ask for whatsoever, and get whatsoever here and now!

The Promises of John. Since the vast majority of the grandiose promises made by Jesus, that Pentecostals like to leverage, are captured by the Apostle John in both his gospel and in his first epistle, let us focus on these. Besides the promise noted above in John 14:13-14, John records four other similar promises voiced by Jesus, and they are all part of the discourse given during the "Last Supper" to our Lord's eleven apostles.

John 15:7 *If you abide in Me, and My words abide in you, ask whatever you wish, and it will be done for you.*

John 15:16 *You did not choose Me but I chose you, and appointed you that you would go and bear fruit, and that your fruit would remain, so that whatever you ask of the Father in My name He may give to you.*

John 16:23 *In that day you will not question Me about anything. Truly, truly, I say to you, if you ask the Father for anything in My name, He will give it to you.*

John 16:24 *Until now you have asked for nothing in My name; ask and you will receive, so that your joy may be made full.*

Again, John chapters 13-17 comprise the discourse at the Last Supper from Jesus to His eleven apostles. Therefore these passages are in a cohesive unit having a single purpose. That purpose was to entice the apostles to see how their Lord wanted to use them and their prayers to continually expand the Kingdom of God throughout the entire church age. For us to inject creature comforts as part of the answers to these promises is outside of their intended purpose.

John 16:25 seems to be the clincher for the true purpose of these grandiose promises since it clarifies that all these precious promises should be viewed with a heavenly perspective or a kingdom focus and not with an earthly focus. It states, "*These things I have spoken to you in figurative language.*"

Clearly, Jesus did not mean to convey that we can ask for any earthly thing imaginable, such as health, wealth, long life, and no persecution, to squander it on our lusts. Rather, we can ask for any heavenly thing (which is what is being 'figuratively' addressed), such as fruit of the Spirit and whatever promotes kingdom growth, so that God can be glorified.

God does not need any of us to be filthy rich for us to accomplish His will. We can be dirt poor, wearing a burlap sack, and eating insects like John the Baptist (Matthew 3:4) and still accomplish everything we need to do for God, with heavenly rewards being credited to our account beyond our wildest imaginations.

Consider this: Mark J. Cartledge says Pentecostalism is largely a religion of the poor, with an estimated 87 percent of Pentecostals living below the poverty line.[14] And what do we see with this materialistic, esoteric, experience-based religion? The top tier echelon reaps the receipts while the poor keep sending in their seed money while expecting everything, but reaping little to nothing in return. No healings and no quick return on investments for the vast majority of contributors. The professional marketers keep chanting their mantra of "Sow your seed of faith to reap your rewards now," and the money keeps rolling in.

God promises to meet our needs and our desires that line up to His will, not our wants. We are told to be content with

---

[14] Mark J. Cartledge, "Pentecostalism," in *The Wiley-Blackwell Companion to Practical Theology* [Chichester, West Sussex, UK: Blackwell, 2012], 587.

just food and clothing (1Timothy 6:8). If we had this kind of attitude we would avoid the greed mentality which God would have to prune out of us with trials and testings.

Think about this – is God more concerned about a family having a comfortable and enjoyable life full of expensive things, or is He more interested in conforming His saints into the image of His Son? If money was a concern to God as much as it is to us, then He would make more of His saints independently wealthy beginning with such faithful servants as the widow with two mites in Mark 2:42-44 and the faithful, but destitute widows of 1Timothy 5.

We know that God does not need any of us rich to accomplish His will. He just wants us dependent on Him and for us to conform to the image of His Son. If money is in the way of achieving this goal God has no problem removing that stumbling block from His children. God is the one that gives us the ability to accumulate wealth (Deuteronomy 8:18).

Prosperity preachers teach a get-rich-quick scheme, which only seems to work for them as they pilfer their constituents. We need to remember God's concept for increasing one's net worth is time plus diligence plus His grace. Positive thinking while wrongly giving to false prophets and false teachers will only deplete a donor's bank account.

⌘

"Wealth hastily gotten will dwindle, but those who gather little by little will increase it" Proverbs 13:11 [NRSV].

⌘

Also, when it comes to deliberately mishandling God's word to reap profits, we all need to be aware of some harsh consequences. Jesus declares in Matthew 5:19 that *"anyone who breaks one of the least of these commandments and teaches others to do the same will be called least in the kingdom of heaven."* So those prosperity preachers and so-called faith healers who profit by twisting the words so carefully authored by the Holy Spirit will receive their reward only on this side of Heaven. For when they transition to eternity they will be the paupers.

Let's continue our line of reasoning of having a proper heavenly focus. A cursory read through John will reveal other passages with a strong heavenly perspective. These include John 2:19, *"Destroy this temple and in three days I will raise it again;"* John 3:3-12 *"You must be born again"*; John 6:27 *"Do not work for the food which perishes but for the food which endures to eternal life"*; and John 6:51-52 *"You must eat my flesh and drink my blood to live."*

Whenever Jesus spoke figuratively it was always to convey a spiritual or heavenly meaning which leads to the "true riches" (Luke 16:11). Examples also include the following passages of Scripture:

Mark 9:45 *"If your foot causes you to stumble, cut it off; it is better for you to enter life lame, than having your two feet, to be cast into hell"* (How many people do you know who cut off their limbs to avoid sin? This is a hyperbolic, or an exaggerated, statement Jesus uses to drive home a hard hitting lesson).

John 6:51 *"...eat my flesh and drink my blood" and you shall live"* (This basically means to hunger and thirst for His righteousness).

John 6:63 *"...The words that I speak to you are spirit, and they are life."* (Again, Jesus is emphasizing a heavenly focus).

Luke 10:19 *"Behold, I have given you authority to tread on serpents and scorpions, and over all the power of the enemy, and nothing will injure."*(The context refers to spiritual entities; *"serpents and scorpions"* equates to demonic entities, so no permanent spiritual or eternal injury is the intent). BUT didn't the apostles get beaten and most died a martyr's death? Recall in 2Corinthians 11:24 that Paul, himself, received 39 lashes five times.

Mark 16:17, 18, 20 *"And these signs shall follow them that believe; In my name shall they cast out devils; they shall speak with new tongues; They shall take up serpents; and if they drink any deadly thing, it shall not hurt them; they shall lay hands on the sick, and they shall recover... And they went forth, and preached everywhere, the Lord working with THEM, and confirming the word with signs following"* [Note that all verbs are in present tense.]

Let's back up to John 15:16 where Jesus states *"that whatever you ask of the Father in My name He may give to you."* The context of this particular chapter from 15:1-16 deals with the Lord's servants producing fruit. This is not a name-it-and-claim-it passage for possessions and positions, but rather a name-it-expect-it promise from God. Pentecostals have a tendency to base many of their doctrines on individual verses without considering the context the verses are contained in. This type of weak hermeneutics will lead to any doctrinal position imaginable.

3. Healings in the Book of Acts and the Epistles

We have one major goal imposed upon us by our Creator according to John 15. We are to produce fruit, and not just a little fruit, but a lot of fruit. This fruit is used to bring glory, credit, and honor to our God. Plus, this fruit is a byproduct of our prayer life – ask and it will be given!

We also need to take notice how many times Jesus repeats His instructions throughout John 15. The repetition drives home the priority and significance of His teachings on this vital subject of praying for MUCH fruit in our lives.

According to the first part of John 15:16, *"You did not choose Me but I chose you, and appointed you that you would go and bear fruit, and that your fruit would remain;"* We are chosen and appointed to bear permanent fruit – which means God is committed to help us bear this fruit. Here is God's commitment: Whatever fruit we ask for – we will get it. This is a name-it-expect-it passage in producing permanent fruit for the Kingdom, and not for seeking individual creature comforts, which are earthly and temporal.

Try asking for more patience and see what happens. Or ask for more witnessing opportunities. We could also ask to grow more in grace and knowledge, or ask for more responsibilities. Few would argue that God loves to answer those kinds of prayers, subjective as they may be, almost on a daily basis.

We should also consider Psalms 5:3 where in the morning we pray, then we watch expectantly for an answer. The fruit God is looking for is not found in our possessions nor in our position in life, but in the qualities developed in our character (love, joy, peace, patience, kindness, goodness, faithfulness, gentleness, self-control) and in our accomplishments for the Kingdom – souls converted, ministered to, and discipled.

The Apostle Peter is a prime example. Reading through the Gospels we can see that Peter was once quite abrasive. He often spoke or acted first rather than first listening and thinking through a matter. He also didn't seem to care about other people's feelings. He exhibited no patience with people, had no self-control, and didn't mind swinging a sword at someone's head and then fleeing from persecution when the adrenalin apparently subsided.

By the time we get to his later writings in first and second Peter we see a major transformation has occurred in his character traits. He developed into a very gentle, compassionate, patient, and loving man. He taught that our trials in life are precious (1Peter 1:7); we need to be obedient children, not controlled by our former lusts (1Peter 1:14), we need to have sincere and fervent love of the brethren (1Peter 1:22); and it all comes together in 2Peter 1:6-7 where he tells us we need to build up our faith in self-control, patience, godliness, brotherly kindness, and love. Only the power of God through the Holy Spirit can produce such maturity, such fruit in a small amount of time as in one's lifetime.

Pentecostals also teach we should live in a covenant relationship with God. They erroneously confuse the New Testament Church as being under the same covenant relationship as the Israelites. They often quote 1Peter 2:24 and Isaiah 53:5, "*Who bore our sins in his own body on the tree, that we, being dead to sins, should live unto righteousness: by whose stripes we were healed.*" The context, however, is not of physical healing but spiritual healing from our sins, which would condemn us to Hell if we were not healed.

In like fashion, Psalms 103:3 "*Who pardons all your iniquities, who heals all your diseases;*" is often claimed for healings, but again, the context needs to be evaluated for proper interpretation. God truly pardons our iniquities, but we often have to deal with the consequences of our sins throughout our life time. We will enter Heaven without one sin dragging behind us. In like fashion, our ailments will not follow us into Heaven, but that does not mean we won't suffer for years here on earth with various ailments and handicaps by God's direct will. Even Elisha "*became sick with the illness of which he was to die*" (2Kings 13:14). No covenant promise can be claimed for ongoing health issues this side of the future millennial kingdom.

Another great promise often used by continuationists to justify and promote their viewpoint is Matthew 21:21-22 where it states, "*...Truly I say to you, if you have faith and do not doubt, you will not only do what was done to the fig tree, but even if you say to this mountain, 'Be taken up and cast into the sea,' it will happen. And all things you ask in prayer, believing, you will receive.*" Are there any conditions, which have to be met? Does someone need to be righteous? Does the request need to be in line with God's will? Then why didn't Paul get his thorn in the flesh removed? Why couldn't Paul get Epaphroditus immediately healed? Why did Timothy have to take wine/medicine for his "often infirmities"? Why did Paul leave Trophimus sick in Miletus?

Since there are no contradictions in Scripture, we have to acknowledge there are conditions to meet. This is born out very clearly in another promise John provided to us, this time in one of his epistles. 1John 5:14-15 states, *"This is the confidence which we have before Him, that, if we ask anything according to His will, He hears us. And if we know that He hears us in whatever we ask, we know that we have the requests which we have asked from Him."*

Now we clearly see that every request must be in God's will. We have to factor in one of the primary hermeneutic principles – the Principle of Added Clarification, which states if a parallel passage provides more details, the proper interpretation is based on that clarification.

Therefore, after comparing what the Holy Spirit accomplished in Acts with what no longer seems possible in the epistles, we have to acknowledge the Holy Spirit is operating differently than what He did in times past. He is no longer healing ALL. Can this change in mode of operandi be observed in Church history? Absolutely, as we will see in the next chapter. In fact, nothing in the entire New Testament indicates that anyone other than Jesus performed supernatural miracles of nature such as walking on water, turning water into wine, calming the sea, killing a fig tree, catching large droughts of fish, and taking tax money from a fish.

CHAPTER 4
CHURCH HISTORY ON HEALINGS AND MIRACLES

"…do not forget the things which your eyes have seen and they do not depart from your heart all the days of your life; but make them known to your sons and your grandsons." Deuteronomy 4:9

This chapter will look at more defensible arguments for the cessationist position both from Scripture and from historical testimony.

PRECEDENCE OF GOD CHANGING HIS WAYS

God may be the same yesterday, today, and forever from a character perspective, but God does alter His plans for succeeding generations. This is most obvious with the dispensational and covenant theologies derived from Scripture. Everyone will admit that God no longer requires animal sacrifices after the Cross. Can we get a hearty Amen on that one? Another big change we find in the New Testament is that the Holy Spirit now indwells within all of His people. These are just some of the highlights for God changing His ways down through the years.

Another consideration is the cessation of the apostles. By implication, so have the *"signs of an Apostle"* such as spontaneous healings and miracles, prophetic revelations, the penning and confirming of Scripture, and the cessation of the supernatural gifts of the Holy Spirit.

Precedence for Supernatural Miracles Ending. From a supernatural perspective we do not have to go far in the Bible to find ample evidence of God turning off the supernatural switch to suit His will for a particular generation or time period. For example, the Israelites witnessed numerous providential and supernatural miracles during their departure from Egypt and while wondering through the wilderness for 40 years.

Many assume the ten plagues God used to convince the Egyptian Pharaoh to release the Jews were supernatural. The plagues, however, could actually have occurred providentially by God using various natural phenomena. It is possible God used the eruption of Mount Thera on the Greek island of Santorini in the Mediterranean Sea to deliver the plagues on Egypt and even lead to the parting of the Red Sea. This volcanic eruption is archeologically dated around 1500 B.C., which closely dates to the assumed time of the Exodus.

This Mount Thera eruption has been estimated to have been over twenty times bigger than the Mount St Helen's eruption in May 1980. Moreover, from ancient pumice samples taken from the seabed it has been determined that the prevailing winds had been blowing in the direction of Egypt. The Egyptian coast is less than 500 miles from Thera and so it is almost certain the volcanic cloud would have covered much of the country.[15]

Let us walk through the ten plagues and see if they are plausible to be caused by natural occurring phenomena as a result of a volcanic eruption. These plagues are recorded in Exodus chapters seven through eleven. As a comparison, events from the 1980 Mount Saint Helens eruption along with the 1982 eruption of Mount Cameroon in West Africa will be used.

---

[15]http://www.grahamphillips.net/Books/act_new.htm#country

Plague #1 – Water turned to Blood. For weeks after the Mount Saint Helens eruption fish in thousands of miles of rivers were found floating on the surface, killed by chemical pollutants in the water. Many volcanoes have another, more corrosive toxin in their bedrock – iron oxide. After the Mount Saint Helens eruption thousands of tons of iron oxide were discharged into the rivers killing fish for miles around. It would certainly explain the Exodus reference to the Nile turning to blood, as iron oxide would turn the river blood red.

Plagues #2, #3, and #4 – Frogs, Gnats & Insects. As the water toxicity increases in the rivers and lakes amphibians would scamper away, and gnats and insects would multiply and swarm on the bloating carcasses of fish. Nothing supernatural here.

Plague #5 – Egyptian Livestock Die. After Mount Saint Helen's eruption many livestock perished or had to be destroyed due to prolonged inhalation of the volcanic dust. From the Hebrews' perspective, since they were primarily located in the land of Goshen, many miles from the more devastating effects of a Mount Thera eruption affecting Egypt, their livestock were providentially spared from harm.

Plague #6 – Boils. Again, after Mount Saint Helen's eruption hundreds of people, as far away as Billings in Montana, over 500 miles from the volcano, were taken to hospital with sore eyes and skin rashes caused by exposure to the acidic fallout ash. Following the 1982 eruption of Mount Cameroon in West Africa survivors succumbed to blisters and boils over large parts of their body.

Plague #7 – Hail mixed with Fire. Volcanic atmospheric conditions are known to induce icy hail along with falling fiery embers.

Plague #8 – Locusts. Prevailing ash-laden winds coupled with icy hail and falling embers and debris would drive migrating locusts, which are already common to the area, to amass on land in more concentrated numbers.

Plague #9 – Darkness. After the Mount Saint Helens eruption the sun was obscured for hours over 500 miles from the volcano.

Plague #10 –The firstborn of the Egyptians and beast die. The 1982 eruption of Mount Cameroon killed hundreds in their sleep from seepage of carbon dioxide gas that was concentrated close to the ground suffocating those in bed, and then the gas dissipated harmlessly into the atmosphere. In ancient Egypt, the first born have the privilege of sleeping on a bed often close to the ground, while their siblings either slept on rooftops or other platforms higher off the ground. What were the Israelites doing in the evening hours? They were up and about, young and old, celebrating the first Passover meal, and packing to leave.[16] They would not have been bothered by the odorless, colorless, suffocating carbon dioxide.

If God used natural phenomena for the 10 plagues, where were the supernatural miracles of the Exodus? It is plausible God used His sovereign control over nature to providentially force the hand of the Pharaoh to release the Hebrews, and

---

[16] History Channel documentary, The Exodus Decoded, 2006

God reserved supernatural works only for the benefit of His Hebrew children.

Was the burning bush that God used to attract Moses' attention, which was not consumed, a supernatural work or a natural phenomenon? Unless God planted the bush over a natural occurring gas vent and it was the gas that burned and not the bush, we can assume the burning bush was a supernatural work. We can also assume that the transformation of Moses' rod into a snake was a supernatural wonder, while the snake-rods of the magicians were probably "lying wonders."

God's Sovereignty. Assuming God did use the eruption of Mount Thera on the island of Santorini to kick off the events of the Hebrew Exodus means God pre-programmed that geological event to occur even before the world was created. How incredible is that? And He accomplished His will for the Hebrew children without turning anyone, including the Pharaoh, into a mindless robot. A study of God's sovereignty would take a series of books just to scratch the surface. Suffice it to say that the Exodus ordeal actually gives us confidence that the events foretold in the book of Revelation will happen just as they are laid out as well. Nothing has or will take God by surprise, and He has every event under His full authority.

Remember what typically constitutes a supernatural wonder from our human perspective. It is one of three possibilities: 1) God used a known natural law, principle, or material to accomplish an unusual result; or 2) perhaps God used a law of nature that has not yet been discovered or is simply beyond human understanding at this moment; or

3) perhaps what happened cannot be described by any natural law because God chose to suspend or violate a natural law.

Everyone has a story or has heard of stories of supposed supernatural miracles. And there are some stories which are very hard to explain. In one story, a mother was walking down the street with her toddler. Then, for unknown reasons, the toddler let go of her mother's hand and darted out into the busy street. The mother could only close her eyes fully expecting a fast approaching car to kill her daughter. When she opened her eyes after the screeching of brakes had stopped, her daughter was seen on the other side of the street safe and sound. How did she get there so fast without getting hit? The driver of the car who nearly hit the girl said he saw someone pick her up in the nick of time and put her down over on the other side. But no guy was standing nearby. Was it an angel? Was this a supernatural event? Were any laws of time, material, and space broken to prevent this girl from getting hit and possibly killed? If so, why save this girl and let so many other children die on the streets each year? As you can see we have more questions than answers, and, as usual, everything is very subjective.

Scripture does say we will entertain angels without realizing it (Hebrews 13:2). Was this one of them? We can only speculate, and yes, God still gets the glory. But Christians are not the only ones who can testify to such stories. Mormons, Buddhists, Muslims and countless other faiths have similar stories of their own. Since speculation is the norm in such stories, we can only take it at face value without pronouncing yea or nay if it was truly of God or not.

Remember, if we cannot prove an incident to be true, we are not obligated to believe it.

We probably have all heard stories about seemingly miraculous or at least providential events that saved lives on that infamous day called 9/11 in 2001. I need to add one more story of how my wife, Karen, and our good friend from Harrogate, England, Janet Brewster, survived that fateful morning as they headed for the Twin towers and the Statue of Liberty for a day of site-seeing. At that time, Karen and I were living near Washington, D.C. Janet made plans to fly to the U.S. to visit with us, and make a few day trips around the area with Karen, including to New York City. It so happened they scheduled a trip to New York on 9/11 with the highlight being a tour through the World Trade Center (WTC) buildings beginning around 9:00 am. They made their flight arrangements from Baltimore Washington Airport (BWI) to New York. They planned to be at the WTC complex before 9:00 that morning, or so they thought. The first plane hit the North Tower at 9:03 AM, with the South Tower getting hit 17 minutes later. At 9:59 AM the South Tower was the first of the two buildings to fall.

When the airline ticket agent asked which airport Karen and Janet preferred to fly into, she was unable to advise them which would work out best for their site-seeing plans. At that time a woman came up to the counter and stated they would enjoy the commute from Islip Airport better than La Guardia. So they bought tickets to Islip to arrive by 8:30 the next morning. It was just a one hour flight. When they arrived in Islip they realized they were still at least an hour away from the twin towers and had to buy train tickets to get there a little after 9:30. Although frustrated they took it in stride, not knowing that this had kept them from being right in the middle of the chaos that was about to unfold near La Guardia airport.

As they neared the World Trade Center they heard a woman yelling, "Suicide! Suicide? He did what?" The porter just then told them a plane had hit the World Trade Center and many people were feared dead. Karen and Janet were stunned and frankly didn't know what to do. Not long after that they heard a second plane had hit the other tower. Their train slowed and stopped on the tracks. They were in viewing distance of the towers and saw the smoke rising from the buildings. The towers appeared as smoke stacks in the distance. The decision was made to turn the train around.

Upon arriving in the city of Jerico, New York a woman turned in her seat and recommended to Karen and Janet to stay in Jerico for the night. She got them a taxi and took them to the closest hotel, and they obtained the last room available. They were now staying in New York for the night without luggage, or the ability to communicate with family members, so they anxiously watched the TV until they could no longer stay awake. The next morning, as they were figuring out how to get back to Maryland, they heard that all planes were grounded but the train station remained open.

At the train station a woman came up to them and asked, "Are you going to DC?" and she kindly escorted them through the chaos at the train station to the area they needed to purchase tickets. She hugged them and said God is watching over you. They were surprised at her statement but knew it to be true. When Karen and Janet entered the area there were literally hundreds of people trying to get train tickets, so they chose a random line and waited. In about five minutes they realized they were at a kiosk where they could buy tickets with a credit card. They bought their tickets and sat down to wait. In about five minutes a man (not in any uniform) told them, "You are going to DC. There is a train leaving from Gate 14 in ten minutes. Be on it." Karen informed him they had tickets for noon. He said all tickets were being honored.

So, they decided to check it out, but actually discussed that the man probably just wanted their seats. When they arrived at Gate 14 no train and no one was around. A few minutes later a porter came by and they asked him if he knew about a train at Gate 14. He checked, came back and said that it had not been announced yet but, yes, the train could be boarded. He escorted them to the train. The ladies were the first ones on it. They arrived back in the Washington D.C. area in relative ease compared to most others who were caught up in that tragedy. As they departed the train a woman came up to them and asked if they needed to find the subway station. She kindly directed them through the station to find the subway station to get to Maryland. When they arrived in Maryland, they were within 2 miles of home. A lone taxi waited in the line. They were home by noon. Not only had God's providence protected them, they felt they were guided every step of the way.

Did Janet and Karen deserve such favored treatment from God, who just hours before allowed 3,000 other souls to perish horribly, with many others scarred for life? No, but we were all grateful for His unmerited grace.

Miraculous Epochs. By providentially using natural events instead of violating His established physical laws of the universe to work miracles and wonders, God allows skeptics and non-believers to have wiggle room not to be forced to believe in Him. It is not that God doesn't work supernatural healings and miracles, but He limits them to specific periods of history and to specific individuals for specific reasons. This is clearly born out in Scripture. There seems to be about five epochs or time periods of supernatural wonders. These are depicted below:

	Event	Time Period	Duration
1	Creation	~4000 B.C.	6 days
2	Moses, Joshua, and the Exodus	~1340-1300 B.C.	~40 years
3	Elijah and Elisha	~880-840 B.C.	~40 years
4	Jesus and His apostles	~30-70 A.D.	~40 years
5	Revelation 11 (2 witnesses)	After 2000 A.D.	~1,260 days

Back to the Exodus. Supernatural wonders of God were definitely in evidence before the Hebrew people on a daily basis. They were led by a column of smoke by day and a pillar of fire by night. They were given manna six days each week with enough on the sixth day for its consumption on the seventh day. Their clothes and sandals did not wear out the entire 40 years they wandered in the wilderness. Yet, God prepared them for the day those supernatural miracles would cease and be replaced by more natural-occurring, sovereignly-controlled "providential" miracles, which are more subjective by their nature.

These daily supernatural miracles ended for the Israelites as they crossed the Jordan River. Once in the Promised Land they would now live by faith, not by sight – and they had to convey to the younger generation that God is still the same, as depicted in Deuteronomy 4:9, but He will now operate differently – via providence. When they crossed the Jordan River, their daily free meals of manna immediately came to an end, their clothes and sandals began to wear out; and God's explicit leading by His Angel and by fire & smoke stopped abruptly.

It is noted throughout the book of Joshua that God destroyed the Canaanites and established Israel in the Promised Land through providential battles, weather phenomena such as hailstones, geological phenomena such as earthquakes, and the hardening of enemy hearts.

Supernatural miracles, such as the sun going back 10 degrees during Isaiah's prophetic time period, the fiery ordeal in Daniel, and the wonders from the time of Gideon and Samson, with often 100's of years of separation, are so few and sporadic they should not be construed as something God normally does either then or now. Even those miraculous wonders were given to specifically endowed individuals to accomplish specific God given missions, and they were not given to people at large.

Several years ago a friend of mine asked me and several others to make a trip to West Virginia to help a family member put a new roof on her house. We had the old shingles off, and we also had to take off some plywood because of rot. I was standing on the roof looking down through the rafters into one of the bedrooms and hoping it wasn't going to rain.

And guess what? One of those freak summer rain storms was sweeping over the West Virginia mountains heading straight for us. We started to panic because we had no tarp and not enough time to cover up the roof. As we were scurrying around doing what we could we witnessed a jaw-dropping incident. The rain split before it got to our house. It was raining on the right side of the house and on the left side, and we were dry in the middle. A car rolled down the street and came to a stop in front of the house. The drive yelled out to us and said, "Do you guys see this? It's raining in front of my car and behind my car, and I'm parked in the only dry spot."

Some of the guys on the roof said let's go down and get the wives and let them see this unusual sight. They found the wives praying in one of the bedrooms asking the Lord for us to be able to finish the roof before the rain came. We finished the roof with barely a drop of rain on us. Was it a miracle? To us it was since we believed God intervened in answer to the prayers of our wives. Was it a supernatural miracle? No, since no natural laws were broken. God could have sovereignly directed that rain to behave as it did before the world was created, whether the wives prayed or not.

Now, someone could easily challenge me on whether or not that rain phenomenon we experienced in West Virginia was truly a miracle of God. Recall that even Satan can control the weather as seen in the book of Job. They could say that the weather phenomenon we experienced was either coincidental or even of Satan. And they would be right in challenging my experience based on what they know from Scripture. The challenge goes both ways. I can challenge them, and they can challenge me. That is how iron sharpens iron. The word of

God is not in question, but our interpretation of the word of God, and our interpretation of the facts surrounding any experience is always in question.

For anyone to make a claim that a particular weather phenomenon is a miracle of God is always subjective. How many times have we said or heard people say that God answered prayers for rain on the crops, or for no rain at the family reunion picnic, or for snow on Christmas, or for a tornado to miss the house? We can still give God the praise for answering such prayers, but it could easily have been coincidental. In other words, the weather was going to behave the way it did whether we prayed for it or not. No skeptic would be forced to believe.

Can Satan control the weather? According to Scripture, the answer is Yes – with God's permission, of course. He apparently used a tornado-like event to destroy the house where Job's children were residing one day, killing all ten of them in the process. We also see in Revelation 13 where Satan empowers the second beast (i.e., the False Prophet) to call fire down from the sky on command (possibly lightning). We, therefore, cannot convince anyone beyond a reasonable doubt that any particular weather phenomena was a direct answer by God to a prayer we or someone else uttered, except for those already noted in Scripture.

Miracles between Then and Now. Looking at miracles since the time of the apostles we see a notable change. Yes, miracles are noted to have occurred throughout church history, and occurred in abundance at times. Historical miracles after the first century include stories of healings, prophecies, visions, speaking in tongues, walking on water, and even resurrections, but they are very subjective with little to no collaborating evidence. Even modern missionary stories of the miraculous are very subjective based on questionable second and third hand information.

In this day of cameras, videos, and social media, any miracle should easily be captured, widely disseminated, and verified. And some have. But even those which have been recorded have been very subjective with no definitive proof of a supernatural miracle occurring. If God were performing supernatural healings and miracles today, with video and internet technologies being available, even captured and posted events would be questioned as possible video fraud. That is okay since we are commanded to prove all things according to Scripture, and only hold fast to that which definitively passes the test.

Testimony from Early Church Fathers. Tongues are not mentioned at all by the post-apostolic Fathers. These men included Polycarp of Smyrna (c. 69-155 AD), Ignatius of Antioch (c. 35-117 AD), and Clement of Rome (died 99 AD). Other later writers such as Justin Martyr (c. 100-165 AD), Origen (c. 184-254 AD), Chrysostom (c. 344-407 AD), and Augustine (c. 354-430 AD) considered tongues as something that happened only in the earliest days of the Church. Chrysostom's position best sums up the considerable evidence from the early church fathers that the age of miracles was over.

Irenaeus (~140-200 AD), a disciple of Polycarp, who was a disciple of the Apostle John, refers to prophecies and healings as present in his time, but resurrections from the dead are placed in past tense. Augustine, who interpreted much of

Scripture allegorically instead of literally, affirmed the continuation of miracles, but few today would acknowledge any of his reports as genuine[17]

Robert Saucy says this about proving supernatural wonders: "The fact that historical evidence has been used for both positions (cessationism and continuationism) points to the difficulty of its interpretation. Even today, so in the past it is difficult to distinguish a genuine miracle from a spurious or even a demonic one....[so] it seems impossible to deny that miraculous activity of the quality and extent associated with the era of Christ and the apostles is not found as a continuing phenomenon in the later church."[18]

The Expositor's Bible Commentary has this to say about the early Corinthian church, "The passing of the apostles and the incidence of heresy and pseudo-charismatic excesses compelled the church to tackle this issue of ecclesiastical order and discipline by the turn of the first century. In A.D. 96 Clement of Rome wrote a lengthy letter reprimanding the Christians in Corinth who had deposed their elders. Since these leaders had been appointed on apostolic authority as well as by common consent, they were not to be regarded as dispensable."[19]

---

[17]Wayne G. Grudem, general editor. (1996). *Are Miraculous Gifts for Today*. Grand Rapids: Zondervan, 116.

[18]Ibid, 113.

[19] The Expositor's Bible Commentary, 589.

CHURCH HISTORY AS CAPTURED BY B. B. WARFIELD

While doing research on miracles one resource that kept getting referenced frequently by other authors was *Counterfeit Miracles* by Benjamin Breckinridge Warfield.

B. B. Warfield (Nov 5, 1851 – Feb 16, 1921) was professor of theology at Princeton Seminary from 1887 to 1921. Some conservative Presbyterians consider him to be the last of the great Princeton theologians before the split in 1929 that formed Westminster Theological Seminary and the Orthodox Presbyterian Church.

Warfield's *Counterfeit Miracles* is actually a compilation of a series of lectures he presented to students at the Columbia Theological Seminary, Columbia, South Carolina in October 1917. He addressed the historicity and the validity of many miracles, which have occurred throughout church history.

In brief, Warfield makes a distinction between the miracles of the Apostolic age, which are "beyond nature" with those of the post Apostolic era called "ecclesiastical" miracles, which are acknowledged by faith-healers of all ages to be inferior to those of the Apostolic era. Warfield also makes a compelling case that supernatural Apostolic miracles ceased even before the apostles died off, and what the church has been experiencing since are providential miracles at best, demonic "lying wonders" at worst, but not supernatural miracles.

Many of the challenges Warfield witnessed regarding faith-healers of his era are the same we see in our era – they are very subjective; many attested to incomplete healings; more grandiose healings are based on hearsay and unsubstantiated claims; and many healings are attributed to those promoting false teachings.

Warfield states that "theologians of the post-Reformation era…taught with great distinctness that the charismata ceased with the Apostolic age."[20] He also summed up historical findings since the Apostolic era: "When we come to think of it, it is rather surprising that the Christians had no raisings from the dead to point to through all these [post Apostolic] years. The fact is striking testimony to the marked sobriety of their spirit. The heathen had them in plenty."[21]

Norman Geisler and Frank Turek, in their book *I Don't Have Enough Faith to Be an Atheist,* give evidence that heathens had no resurrection stories that paralleled a dying and rising god until 150 A.D., more than 100 years after the origin of Christianity. The only known account of a god surviving death that predates Christianity is the Egyptian cult god Osiris. In this myth, Osiris is cut into fourteen pieces, scattered around Egypt, then reassembled and brought back to life by the goddess Isis. Osiris, however, does not actually come back to physical life, but becomes a member of a shadowy underworld. So if there was any influence of one on the other, it was the influence of the historical event of the New Testament on mythology, not the reverse.[22]

---

[20]Warfield, B. B. (Originally Published 1918, Republished 2012). *Counterfeit Miracles.* New York: Charles Scribner's Sons (1918) and Forgotten Books (2012), 3.

[21]Ibid, 15.

[22] Norman L. Geisler and Frank Turek, *I Don't Have Enough Faith to Be an Atheist,* (Crossway Books, Wheaton, Illinois, 2004), 312

The testimony of the early church fathers convey that miracles ceased with the Apostolic age. Yet miracles of a lesser sort ("ecclesiastical miracles") were still occurring during their lifetimes, but these miracles are ascribed to a saint's tomb or relics, or even the Eucharist. In other words these lesser miracles are attributed to the worship of relics.[23]

Warfield was complimentary of Augustine, except when it came to miracles. Warfield acknowledged that Augustine was incomparably the greatest man whom the Church possessed "between Paul the Apostle and Luther the reformer." Augustine was called "Augustine the Truthful." Yet, Warfield stated, "Whenever it is a case of marvelous happenings, he [Augustine] shows himself quite unreliable" believing unsubstantiated miracles and expecting his readers to do the same."[24]

Warfield also quotes Augustine about a "considerable number of [miracles] were wrought by the relics of the 'most glorious martyr, Stephen'" whose bones had come to light in Jerusalem in 415. Almost 70 miracles in less than two years were ascribed to the Stephen's shrine in Hippo, who acquired fragments in 424.[25]

Warfield also stated, "It was naturally a source of embarrassment to Augustine that heretics had miracles to appeal to just like his own; and that the heathen had had

---

[23]Warfield, B. B. (Originally Published 1918, Republished 2012). Counterfeit Miracles. New York: Charles Scribner's Sons (1918) and Forgotten Books (2012), 46-51.

[24]Ibid, 76-78.

[25]Ibid, 38.

something very like them from time immortal."[26] Warfield, however, did latch on to one statement that Augustine made which has proven quite true down through the ages. Augustine pointed out that the connection of alleged miracles with erroneous doctrines invalidates their claim to be genuine works of God.[27] Another way to put it is that experience does not determine biblical truths; rather biblical truth judges each and every experience.

Fortunately, God does not wait till all of our doctrines and attitudes are 100% perfect before He considers answering our prayers? If so, then none of us would be worthy of God's attention with the exception of Jesus. Most would agree, however, that the core teachings of Scripture must be faithfully adhered to before God would put His seal of approval by granting a supernatural miracle by the hands of His people.

Now, how do we judge the miracles of Lourdes, France? Catholics lay claim that the healings which occur at Lourdes are genuine works of God and they, therefore, confirm Catholic doctrine as being sanctioned from God. Protestants, on the other hand, would say those healings are psychosomatic at best since the Catholic doctrine of Mary, being a co-redeemer with Jesus, abrogates sound biblical doctrine, and God would not be behind such miracles.

With the Catholic Church's proclamation in 1954 of the Immaculate Conception of Mary, Lourdes became the greatest

[26]Ibid, 43.

[27]Ibid, 53.

healing shrine in the world, counting pilgrims in the hundreds of thousands and even millions on an annual basis. During the 20 years between 1888 and 1907 the number of cures recorded at Lourdes was 2,665, yielding a yearly average of 133. One cure for every 1,250 visitors who were looking for a healing was calculated – a paltry number (less than 0.1%) when you consider that Christ and His apostles had a 100% success rate as seen in the Gospels and Acts.

Many healings at Lourdes were partial healings. Warfield recorded Bertrin's medical findings "that it is quite common for traces of the infirmity to remain…[which supposedly keeps] the cured person in grateful memory of the benefit received."[28]

Why should miracles show limitations? As Warfield stated so emphatically "miracles should not carry the doctrine, but the doctrine the miracles."[29] Warfield stated that "the miracles of the 19th century (e.g., Lourdes) recall those of the 3rd century."[30] If we were to compare what we see in our day and age by so-called faith healers we would also put them into the same gallery as those of Lourdes.

Warfield had more to say about miracles which surrounded relic worship: "This great stream of miracle-working (attributed to relics of saints) which has run thus throughout the history of the church was not original to the church, but entered it from without" (via heathenism). [and]

---

[28]Ibid, 108.

[29]Ibid, 123.

[30]Ibid, 76.

"The more miraculous a story the more readily it found believing acceptance… [and Christians] no longer knew how to distinguish between truth and falsehood."[31] Warfield goes on to say "what we find, when we cast our eye over the whole body of Christian legends, growing up from the 3rd century down through the Middle Ages, is merely a reproduction, in Christian form, …the legends of heathendom."[32] I believe Warfield would say the same thing today if he saw the faith healers of our era.

One more notable comment by Warfield: "The great majority of the miracles of healing which have been wrought throughout the history of the church, have been wrought through the agency of relics…the actual graves of the saints…[even] fragments of their bodies, however minute…have become healing shrines."[33] Protestants may not flock to any healing shrines with entombed relics of saints, but the miracles being touted by non-Catholic faith healers are on the same caliber as our Catholic friends. There is no difference to claim.

What is shocking about relic worship is that the relic does not even need to be genuine to work. Warfield documented that the relics of St. Rosalia at Palermo are really the bones of a goat, and yet they still cured diseases and epidemics.[34]

---

[31]Ibid, 74.

[32]Ibid, 83.

[33]Ibid, 98.

[34]Ibid 268.

Healings and Miracles are Temporary

Some might say, "A healing is a healing no matter if it is relic-related or psychosomatic." Who can argue that, especially if a person walks away even 50% better than before? From a Christian perspective, however, we are to prove all things and hold on to those elements of our faith which are true, and discard elements which could deceive and manipulate us away from God's truth.

If someone's spouse or child had a debilitating or terminal illness, who wouldn't drag them to any device, medication, therapy, or even to a do-gooder who could offer a real cure? That would be our "flesh" side talking. From our "spirit" or "faith" side we would have to consider the "God factor." Where is God in our trials and what is His solution to our problem? Like Job, our faith should be strong enough to accept "evil from the hand of God as well as good," and we should have a long-term spiritual perspective instead of a short-term earthly perspective.

When it comes to physical ailments, there is no such thing as a permanent miracle or healing. Even if someone were raised from the dead, he or she would die of something else later on. We must realize that all healings and miracles which are of God have a short-term purpose – to point people to God and to provide temporary comfort.

In Luke 4:18-21 Jesus read Isaiah 61:1, the passage which proclaimed His purpose on earth, 1) To preach the Gospel to the poor; 2) proclaim release to the captives; 3) give sight to the blind; 4) set free the oppressed; and 5) proclaim the year of the Lord. Then He concluded His speech by stating that, "*This*

Scripture has been fulfilled." He did not say "it is being fulfilled" or "will be fulfilled" but it "has been fulfilled." Jesus was very explicit, and His audience knew what He meant by it.

When Jesus and His apostles and disciples worked their 100% healings and other signs and wonders, it was to fulfill that particular prophecy of Scripture for that appointed time in history. There is no indication in Scripture that such supernatural wonders would continue throughout the church age.

Remember, the Holy Spirit turns on and off the power to work supernatural miracles at His discretion. The Holy Spirit does not work whimsically, but within specific historical time frames, covenants, or dispensations. Luke 5:17 reads "*...and the power of the Lord was with Jesus to heal*" while 1Corinthians 12:11, reads "*But one and the same Spirit works all these things, distributing to each one individually just as He wills.*"

Even Judas, the son of perdition, was presumably able to work miracles and cast out demons since he was specifically endowed with power from God just like the other apostles. Therefore, someone doesn't even need to be extra holy to work miracles. They just need to be specifically empowered by the Holy Spirit during a period of time that fits within God's will for the ages, such as for the Apostolic era and for the era of the two witnesses depicted in Revelation 11.

The True Purpose of Healings & Miracles

When we see supernatural healings and miracles, which are temporary by nature, as a means to make our earthly life more comfortable we miss God's true purpose for such wonders. Many Jews looked at Jesus simply as a miracle-vending machine. All they needed to do was to approach Him or even touch His cloak to receive a personalized healing that was instantaneous and complete.

Admittedly, some of the Jews had the right attitude toward Jesus. They approached Him respectfully, though their faith might have been weak, and Jesus healed them. Jesus even healed those with no faith or with selfish attitudes.

Jesus did draw the line in several cases. He scolded one person, recorded in John 4:48, that "*unless you people see signs and wonders, you simply will not believe.*" In another passage (John 6:26) Jesus again scolded those looking for another miracle, "*...you seek Me, not because you saw signs, but because you ate a free meal*" – and He refused to answer their request for another free meal.

Some might think Jesus possibly contradicted Himself since Matthew 5:42 records Jesus stating we are to "*give to him who asks of you, and do not turn away from him who wants to borrow from you.*" So, why didn't Jesus give to those who asked of Him? We must realize this is one of those negating principles. We are not obligated to give to those who have the means to help themselves, or who are being prodigal, or who are just taking advantage of our goodness. As Paul says, if they don't work, they don't eat (2Thessalonians 3:10). There is a saying in the counseling arena that the first time you render aid to someone asking for help it is called mercy, the second time you help it is called enabling.

Psalms 106:15 paints a very ugly picture of what happens when God answers prayers He doesn't want to answer. This passage references what happened to the Jews during the Exodus when they selfishly wanted more than what God had desired for them to have (See Numbers 11). The Jews cried for meat to eat instead of the steady supply of manna God had so richly provided.

And he gave them their request; but sent leanness into their soul.
Psalms 106:15

When our attitude toward God is "what can I get from Him today" then we have totally missed it just like the Jews of the Exodus and the Jews who sought for one more sign from Jesus. Jesus performed countless healings and miracles, yet John 12:37 records that many still did not believe in Him even after all the supernatural wonders He had done. This incident in John is reminiscent of what happened with the Jews of the Exodus who ate the quail, for Psalms 78:32 records, "*in spite of all this, they kept on sinning; in spite of his wonders, they did not believe.*"

When Pentecostals keep praying for supernatural healings and miracles, which are not of God's will (according to the cessationist' view), they open themselves up to receiving deceptive healings and possibly other "lying wonders" from Satan, with God's permission, of course, as leanness to their souls.

Pentecostals may even give God the credit, but it is credit God does not want or desire because His will was opposed. I have lost count of how many Pentecostal friends and acquaintances I have seen drop out of church because the god they had created in their own image did not meet their wants, desires, and perceived needs.

On one side of the fence we see supernatural wonders in Scripture, even the raising of the dead (Luke 16:31), that do not entice anyone to accept Christ as Lord. Yet, on the other side of the fence, Scripture does say in several places that many came to the Lord as a result of witnessing or hearing about supernatural events. Recall that many believed after witnessing Lazarus' resurrection (John 11:45) and others came to believe after hearing about his resurrection (John 12:11). Supernatural miracles definitely had a purpose to turn heads and hearts toward Christ – but in the end, people believe what they want to believe. Those who have ears to hear, will hear (Matthew 11:15).

If only we could be more like the Samaritans who believed in Christ after they heard Him (John 4:39-42) and not after they saw something. Their belief was based on substantiated faith and not on sight. They had sufficient information to make an intelligent decision. Whose faith, do you think, would be stronger – those who trusted the truthful and eternal words of Christ, or those who witnessed a temporary shock-and-awe wonder?

Again, the true purpose of Jesus' mission was to fulfill Scripture. Jesus healed ALL who were ill and who came to Him to fulfill what was spoken through Isaiah the prophet: *"He himself took our infirmities and carried away our diseases"* (Matthew 8:16-17). His primary purpose was to teach and preach God's truth. Luke 4:44 records that *"the crowds were searching for Him, and came to Him and tried to keep Him from going away from them. But He said to them, "I must preach the kingdom of God to the other cities also, for I was sent for this purpose."* Therefore, Jesus kept on preaching in the synagogues throughout Judea.

KEY QUESTIONS ON APOSTLES, SATAN, AND PROVIDENCE

Do We Have Apostles Today?

Let us revisit the question, "Do we still have apostles today" like Peter and Paul? Catholics say YES as found in their current Pope. Mormons say YES since they have twelve apostles of their own. Apostolic churches say YES since they have so-called apostles in all their churches. BUT, none of these so-called apostles within these denominations and sects have ever worked the true "*signs of an apostle*."

If apostles, men such as Peter and Paul, still exist today, then, YES, we would conceivably have miracles of the same caliber we see in the Gospels and in Acts. Or at least they would give us definitive and canonical teachings on why or why not, since Scripture would be able to grow beyond the 66 books we currently have. If, however, apostles have ceased, then, arguably, so has supernatural healings, miracles, prophecies, and gifts.

If we think about it, there would be ramifications for having true apostles of Christ existing today. Scripture does differentiate between the Twelve Apostles of Christ and other men designated as apostles of the church; emissaries such as Barnabas, Silas, Epaphroditus, James, the Lord's brother, and others.

If apostles of Christ do exist today (men such as Peter and Paul), then we should see the "signs of an apostle" today.

These include the following: 1) confirmation of being handpicked and taught by Jesus Christ as Paul was; 2) spontaneous miracles and instantaneous healings; 3) confirmed resurrections, even after burial or embalming; 4) the ability to bestow the Holy Spirit on others; and 5) the ability to pen and confirm Scripture (even Apostolic emails and tweets would be collected).

Instead, what we see today is nothing more than providential or psychosomatic healings of "functional disorders" at best, demonic deception at worst. So-called supernatural healings are very subjective with no validation or confirmation. The harder cases involving "organic disorders" (e.g., missing limbs, broken bones, genetic abnormalities, etc.) are never healed of their true lameness, blindness, or sickness.

More Evidence to Consider

There are over 35,000 books dealing with miracles, according to Amazon.com. If any of those supposed miracles recorded in any of those books had any bite of biblical truth in them, we would see people surrounding the healer in very large numbers – whole towns like they did to Jesus, (Mark 6:31 – "*there were so many people coming and going that they (Jesus and His apostles and disciples) did not even have time to eat.*"

Like Jesus, the healer would toil into the late hours healing all those who came for a healing touch. He or she wouldn't just conduct an hour-long service and leave without ensuring everyone got healed who sought for a healing.

Biblical healers would also have the ability to transfer their powers to followers, like Jesus did to His apostles and disciples; and 100% healings and miracles would continue unabated (Luke 9:1; 10:1, 9, 17). Any exceptions, such as being unable to heal the likes of Timothy, Trophimus, and Epaphroditus, would be a rarity and not the norm.

Statistical Evidence

Since the Lord's Church was to grow like a mustard seed or as leaven, this would be exponential growth. So, if supernatural miracles and gifts are truly still with the church today, let us do some simple math using the following inputs:

- The Bible records at least 40 supernatural miracles by Jesus and His disciples over a forty-year period. That is an average of one miracle a year (Let us be very conservative for the sake of argument).
- Also, since Jesus sent out 70 disciples to work miracles, and there were 500 disciples mentioned who witnessed the life of Christ, that is a 14% healer-to-disciple ratio, but let's round it down to 10% to keep it conservative.
- That equates to about one person working one miracle during their 40 year adult lifespan (Again, we are being very conservative).
- With about seven billion people in the world today, statistics show there are over 2 billion Christians, with one-half billion being Pentecostals and Charismatics.
- A 10% healer ratio would mean over 200 million Christians could work supernatural healings and miracles. That means at least 200 million eye-popping miracles should have been performed in the past 40 years, which is one true supernatural miracle

performed by one healer per year, by our conservative calculations.

Consider this – there are more than 18,000 hospitals throughout the world. If each hospital has 100 beds, then there are over 1,800,000 hospital beds that can be occupied at any one time. With more than 200 million eye-popping miracles over 40 years, that equates to five million miracles a year. That is enough supernatural miracles not only to empty every hospital throughout the world each year several times over, but to restore the missing limbs of every amputee over the past 40 years, along with healing every Down Syndrome child worldwide. Yet, there is no confirmed record of any amputee from any era since the time of Christ having their limbs supernaturally restored, or any Down Syndrome child being miraculously healed, much less the emptying out of even one burn ward or one cancer ward of any hospital anywhere.

Therefore, do we have a problem with a lack of faith, or has God moved away from supernatural healings and miracles? Some might say that there are supernatural claims galore around the world; then, why do we have trouble confirming even one, if theoretically, there are more than five million supernatural miracles potentially being worked each year? With Pentecostals and Charismatics accounting for 25% of all Christians, or roughly 500 million, we would expect at least one valid supernatural miracle of some sort should have been verified by now since Pentecostals have been recognized as existing for over the past 100 years.

Even though Pentecostals and Charismatics are acclaimed to be the fastest growing religious segment in the world, numerical growth does not equate to spiritual correctness, righteousness or integrity. Even Mormons at one time were once considered the fastest growing religious segment, but their beliefs in multiple gods and the denial of the Trinity falls outside the pale of Christianity. From this, we need to realize a religious group does not have to have sound doctrine to be large and fast growing. Buyer, beware.

Now we still have to come to grips with the so-called supernatural healings and miracles so many modern faith healers and miracle workers keep touting. The tough part is realizing that in the last days what will Satan do to the world? He will attempt to deceive people with the means of miracles. Recall that Matthew 24:24-26 states, *"For false christs and false prophets will arise and will show great signs and wonders, so as to mislead, if possible, even the elect."* Therefore, we have a priority in our day and age to be skeptical with the miraculous.

Even 2Corinthians 11:14-15 warns us that *"…for even Satan disguises himself as an angel of light. Therefore it is not surprising if his servants also disguise themselves as servants of righteousness."* Is it any surprise that not only secular movies, but even the vast number of Christian television programs, which deal with supernatural healings and miracles, avoid teaching sound doctrine? Whatever glitters and goes "flash and bang" has more commercial selling power than a steady diet of teaching sound biblical principles and commands.

Can Satan Perform Supernatural wonders?

Again, the purpose of satanic wonders is to deceive and destroy. A walk through the Old Testament reveals Satan's abilities and strategies to do harm to mankind. He first appears in Genesis 3 as the "serpent of old" to deceive Eve and cause Adam to sin, and he does it craftily by getting the first couple to doubt God's word.

We soon see the works of the devil in Egyptian sorcerers as they try to challenge Moses by transforming their staffs into snakes (Exodus 7:10-22), but their magic was inferior to God's wonders as Moses' snake swallowed up their snakes.

Can Satan truly perform creative miracles? Remember – the best Satan can do is called "lying wonders" with the purpose to deceive mankind. So, no, Satan cannot create as God can create. In fact, Satan can't do anything without God's specific permission. Satan can only mimic the true works of God, but to our eyes, they will appear quite authentic.

In fact, Satan's wonders are so good that God established the death penalty for those Israelites in the Old Testament who perform divination and witchcraft; interpret omens; work sorcery; cast spells; or who was a medium, a spiritist, or one who calls up the dead (Deuteronomy 18:10-11). The death penalty was also for using enchantments or observing times (astrology), for calling familiar spirits (Leviticus 19:26, 31). False prophets and dreamers whose prophecies and dreams even came true were to be stoned (Deuteronomy 13:1-5). God took such deceptive practices seriously as an affront to His deity and worship and a threat to the truth of His word.

Why would God allow Satan to work such lying wonders and to have the ability to give people such deceptive powers, and, yet, establish the death penalty for those who dabble in such practices? Isn't that entrapment? A probable answer is God did not want His people delving into the meta-physical world because it would lead His people away from Him and ultimately toward Satan. He wanted His people to be firmly grounded in the physical world and in the truth of His word. The miraculous, even from God, was going to be limited, because God wanted to shepherd His people under the natural laws He established for mankind.

We move beyond the Hebrew nation and we find in Scripture the Babylonian magicians performing sorceries and spells that were considered "great power" (Isaiah 47:9), and Nebuchadnezzar had "magicians, conjurers, sorcerers" on his staff to work their skills (Daniel 2:2). Today, there are numerous occult groups in almost every city throughout America, each claiming to work powers of darkness. When you Google satanic miracles it is interesting that all miracles are of the same caliber we see and hear Christian faith healers and miracle workers performing today. People get up out of wheelchairs, cancers are cured, back aches are cured, and even pets are cured of various ailments.

I have a pastor friend who dabbled in the occult before he got saved. He actually doubted the powers of Satan that were promoted by his friends who were into occult practices. On a challenge when he attended his first séance, his prayer to Satan was for Satan to remove an unsightly mole that was on his face. When he woke up the next morning and the mole was gone, it wasn't long before he sought out Christ for a true healing of his soul.

But isn't a healing a healing? To some people, yes, it is. They would rather have a healing from the Devil himself than no healing at all and to live a debilitating and often painful existence. What should a Christian's perspective be on this matter? We should realize that it is better to be a door keeper in the House of God than to dwell in the tents of wickedness (Psalms 84:10), and it is better to take refuge in the LORD than to trust in man (Psalms 118:8). We can faithfully extrapolate that it is better to be blind, lame, or crippled by the hand of God than to receive sight and wholeness from satanic means.

As we move into the New Testament, we see Satan performing more wonders. In Luke 4:6 Satan had power and authority from God and could give it to whomever he wished. We see satanic influence in three passages in the book of Acts. Simon, the magician, in Acts 8:9-19, was called the "Great Power of God" and he astonished people with his sorceries. In Acts 13:6-12 Barjesus or Elymas as he was sometimes called, was a Jewish sorcerer and false prophet. He was blinded by the Apostle Paul for his subtle deceptions and perverse ways. Finally, in Acts 16:16-19 a damsel possessed with a spirit of divination brought her clients much gain until Paul commanded the demon to leave her.

From these passages in Acts we see people having the ability to work sorceries and even to accurately foretell the future for profit. Is it any wonder Christians who think they have the gift of knowledge, or wisdom, or prophecy, tongues, or interpretation of tongues, could actually be conveying information that is available to demons? For example, someone thinking they received a word of knowledge from God about another Christian's sinful past would actually be falling into a demonic trap.

There are two additional comments on Satan's abilities found in Paul's epistles. In 2Corinthians 11:14 Satan is able to disguise himself as an angel of light. Does that mean he can take human form? Only with God's permission, and he will greatly influence two individuals – the Antichrist and the False Prophet, as seen in the book of Revelation. Appearing as an angel of light could take the form of well-meaning intentions. This is seen in Peter telling the Lord with the best of intentions that it would not be proper for Jesus to suffer and die, and Jesus said to Peter, "*Get behind Me, Satan; for you are not setting your mind on God's interests, but man's*" (Mark 8:33). We have to carefully discern God's will through His word to avoid Satan's clever devices to deceive and manipulate.

The second passage in Paul's letters highlighting Satan's abilities to deceive is found in 2Thessalonians 2:9 where he states that "*the coming of the lawless one is according to the working of Satan, with all power, signs, and lying wonders.*" Paul can't be any clearer than this. Satan's powers are real, they look like they are the works of a benevolent God, but their sole purpose is to trip up, to trap, to wound, to kill and destroy, with the ultimate goal to slow down the progress of the Gospel to reach the world for Christ. Consequently, Paul's warning to each of us is to be on our guard and avoid dabbling with anything not of God.

We finally get to the book of Revelation and we find once again that Satan can work tremendous powers through his servants from an apparent resurrection of the Antichrist after he suffered a mortal head wound, to bringing fire out of heaven on command, and working countless other miraculous wonders we can only imagine (Revelation 13:3-14; 19:20). And Satan is not the only one who gets credit for deceiving the masses. His minions ("*spirits of devils*") are also allowed to run about working untold miracles, which probably include healings, manipulation of weather phenomena, battle victories, and a host of other imaginable wonders we often give God the credit for (Revelation 16:14; 18:23).

Benefits of Providential Healings and Miracles

Skeptics over the years have voiced that praying is nothing more than a meaningless crap shoot, a matter of pure chance, a roll of the dice to get a single prayer answered from God. God has been accused of being whimsical and finicky since "He does whatever He pleases" (Psalms 135:6). From a cessationist's perspective, the skeptics have a point since Christians keep praying for instantaneous supernatural healings and miracles, which are no longer part of God's will for us at this time.

We know from the Bible that God is a prayer answering God. He eagerly waits for us to pray so He can positively intervene in our lives to accomplish His will and to receive ultimate glory from the experience. Then how can we get 100% of our prayers answered? After all, Paul tells us in 2Corinthians 1:20 that *"For as many as are the promises of God, in Him they are yes."* In other words, God wants to positively answer our prayers. He does not want to give a "no" answer.

When it comes to praying, we will never go wrong if we search for the answers in the writings of John. As we saw earlier in John, he recorded numerous statements from the lips of Jesus which promised that all of our prayers would be answered positively, no matter what we prayed for, and especially if we stand in agreement with other believers.

John clarifies in 1John 5:14 that our prayers must first be aligned to God's will. Now, from a cessationist's perspective, since it is no longer God's will to heal instantaneously, prayers are altered slightly. For example, a wounded soldier comes home from a war missing a leg, so instead of asking God to restore the man's leg, prayers are focused on dealing with the situation for God's ultimate glory and for all things to work out for the sake of the returning soldier.

That may sound like a cop out, but we need to be like the men of Issachar *"who understood the times, with knowledge of what Israel should do,"* and who became a valuable asset to David as he assumed the leadership over Israel (1Chronicles 12:32). Like the men of Issachar, we need to clearly understand our times, and how God is working in our day and age. This will help us know what to do, when to do it, and how to do it for the glory of God and for the benefit of His Church.

In contrast, the prayers of a continuationist who asked God to restore a man's amputated leg would go unanswered no matter how hard he petitioned God, or how much faith and persistence he mustered up. Even if proof is ever given of just one incident of a limb growing back supernaturally, the infrequency of such an event still would prompt the skeptics to claim "where are the miracles." Therefore, consider praying for God's providential healings and miracles (*"…all things work together for our good"*), then we have a near 100% success rate with our prayers getting positively answered.

One Final Point on Healing the Handicapped

Jesus commands us to do the following according to Luke 14:13-14, "*But when you give a reception, invite the poor, the crippled, the lame, the blind, and you will be blessed, since they do not have the means to repay you; for you will be repaid at the resurrection of the righteous.*" Jesus did not command us to invite the poor, the crippled, the lame and the blind to physically heal them, but to essentially fellowship with them – and to be a source of comfort, a place to feel welcomed and refreshed. Since they would not be able to repay us for such hospitality, means they would not be on their feet (or healed) any time soon.

Another passage that alludes to non-miraculous and non-instantaneous events for our times is Matthew 7:8. This is the passage Jesus used to convey to His disciples to pray for big answers, but to realize persistence will be crucial to get many of our prayers answered.

✦

"For everyone who [keeps asking] receives, and he who [keeps seeking] finds, and to him who [keeps knocking] it will be opened."
Matthew 7:8

✦

It's not that we have to twist God's arm with nagging and repetitive requests to get our prayers answered, but persistence actually helps us adjust our prayers to be more in line with God's will for our particular situation. This approach was probably easier for the Jews of the first century since many had very large portions of Scripture memorized even as youths. We tend to memorize favorite verses scattered throughout the Bible instead of whole passages. A rabbinic student, for example, had the first 12 books of the Old Testament memorized by 12 years of age.

Having Scripture passages within their appropriate context at your fingertips when praying definitely helps to see a situation as God sees it. This explains why Jesus could pray "thy will be done" after He spent considerable time petitioning God to remove the cup of wrath – the Cross, that was before Him (Matthew 26:38-42).

Pentecostals also argue that since Jesus had compassion on those He came across and healed them, one and all, then we should be able to show the same compassion to those needing healings today. That is a nice concept, but observationally and biblically, it is not a reality. Just walk through the corridors of any children's hospital. Where is the compassion of the modern-day faith healers to heal these children? Why aren't they walking these halls to heal each and every one of these young people, some who are fighting terminal illnesses? They are not walking these halls, because – and to be blunt, they cannot heal them. It is not God's will for our day and age for such supernatural healings.

The compassion of God is not at issue, else the compassion of God should have started with preventing a child from coming down with cancer instead of after a child succumbs to this often deadly disease. God is a compassionate God, but His compassion is ultimately reserved, much like His mercy, for specific times. Some of His compassion is seen clearly during the ministry of Christ and His apostles as they went around healing every one of their many and varied ailments. For the rest of us we will realize God's full compassion after we transition out of these mortal shells we call a body.

How long should a sick person be sick? During the time of Christ a person was sick or handicapped for as long as it took them to either gain direct access to Jesus or to have a proxy individual reach Him with their need. If God is truly working the same today as He did with Christ, as Pentecostals claim, then with today's cellular and social networking capabilities, a sick person should only be sick for less than a minute. That is about how long it takes to call a 1-800 prayer line or post a prayer request for a healing onto a social networking site and get a response back. If a person is sick or handicapped beyond the time it takes to send out a prayer request and get a near instantaneous reply then either the wrong person was contacted, or the Internet was down, or God is no longer healing supernaturally.

There are no other alternatives from a Pentecostal faith-healing perspective. If God is seen as the same yesterday, today, and forever having the same compassion as Christ showed to the crowds of the first century, then where are His miracles? That is another core fallacy of the Pentecostal position. Their erroneous belief system collapses around them as the truth of Scripture is revealed.

CHAPTER 5
GIFTS OF THE HOLY SPIRIT – WHAT HAS CHANGED?

But to each one is given the manifestation of the Spirit for the common good. For to one is given the word of wisdom through the Spirit, and to another the word of knowledge according to the same Spirit; to another faith by the same Spirit, and to another gifts of healing by the one Spirit, and to another the effecting of miracles, and to another prophecy, and to another the distinguishing of spirits, to another various kinds of tongues, and to another the interpretation of tongues. But one and the same Spirit works all these things, distributing to each one individually just as He wills.
1Corinthians 12:7-11

The questions often asked about the gifts of the Holy Spirit include: Are all of these gifts supernatural, or only some? Are all of these gifts for the entire church age, or are only some, or none? How can we tell which gifts are still active today, if any, and have they changed?

There are numerous books, blogs, and position papers to read through on every position imaginable on the gifts. Fortunately, Scripture gives us ample evidence to guide us into sorting out what truths we need to have on these gifts.

One caution we should be aware of is we need to be careful taking things either too far or not far enough. We can only go as far as Scripture goes. The Old Testament Scriptures were the only things needed for the Bereans to determine the truth for themselves. Now that we also have the New Testament, we have additional insight from God on the truths we need to investigate and hold on to.

The table below shows the various gifts mentioned in Ephesians, Romans, and 1Corinthians. Of course, many theologians, pastors, and Bible teachers do not consider this list as exhaustive but representative of the various gifts or talents often found within the Church. These gifts are categorized according to their teaching or service function.

Passage	Specific Gifts	Category
Ephesians 4:7, 11-13	Apostle	Teaching
	Prophet	Teaching
	Evangelist	Teaching
	Pastor/Teacher	Teaching
	Grace to all (verse 7)	Service
Romans 12:4-8	Prophecy	Teaching
	Teaching	Teaching
	Grace	Service
	Ministry	Service
	Exhortation	Service
	Giving	Service
	Rules	Service
	Mercy	Service
1Corinthians 12:8-10, 28	Wisdom	Teaching
	Knowledge	Teaching
	Faith	Service
	Gifts of Healings	Service
	Miracles	Service
	Discernment	Service
	Prophecy	Teaching
	Tongues	Teaching
	Interpretation of Tongues	Teaching
	Helps	Service
	Administration	Service

Let's ask ourselves a few questions, and let's first assume that ALL the gifts are still available to the church today. What is the impact to us? Can we tell the difference between someone having the gift of mercy from someone being merciful? Do we have to take a gift survey to determine our gift, or is our gift immediately recognizable at the moment of salvation?

If someone declares they have the gift of administration, do we immediately fire the current church secretary for an unknown, unproven individual? Or, if someone declares they have the gift of teaching, do we immediately make them a Sunday School teacher, or if someone says they are gifted to work with the nursery, should we immediately place them in that demanding position unsupervised? Those are all rhetorical questions with the obvious answer being NO to each of them.

Now let's assume only SOME of the gifts are still active today. What is the impact? Which gifts are still active and why? What happened to the obsolete gifts, and why? How do we tell which gifts are still current or not? And are the gifts still the same as noted in Scripture or have they morphed into something greater or lesser? We will unpack these questions throughout this chapter.

Finally, let's assume NO gifts are active today – what is the impact to the church? How do we biblically articulate that all gifts are obsolete? How do we challenge believers with a different persuasion? How do we respond when some seem to be exercising certain gifts which are obsolete? If false gifts are in existence, how do we prove they are not of God, but are either of Satan, or of the individual's own making? Again, we will need to unpack these questions in the following pages.

No matter what side of the fence we fall on – the left, the right or we split the middle; these are just some of the questions which need to be addressed. If God is a logical and truthful God, which He is, then He should leave ample indications in His word for it to be possible for us to come to the right assumptions and doctrinal positions – and He does. The issues are not problems with God's word, but problems with our interpretation of God's word. We are the fallible creatures. Let God be true and every man a liar (Romans 3:4).

When we get into sensitive discussions with our Pentecostal brothers and sisters we need to remember we are commanded in 2Timothy 2:25 not to be quarrelsome, but to be gentle and patient in our approach, and be able to teach. Our speech, as Paul says in Colossians 4:6 should *"always be with grace, as though seasoned with salt so that we will know how we should respond to each person."* After all, if our speech is salted just right, our listeners should always be thirsty for more information from us. And how can we forget James 1:19 where we need to be *"quick to hear, slow to speak and slow to anger."*

Sometimes, however, even if we come across gently and biblically we can still be accused of being offensive. Even Jesus was accused of having a demon in Him. Let us always be prepared to give the right and timely answer to those who are asking for the hope that lies within us (1Peter 3:5).

Theologians typically slice and dice the gifts up into various categories such as sign gifts, service gifts, prophetic gifts, and a host of other divisions to articulate their diversities or their similarities. The Apostle Peter only refers to two categories of gifts – speaking or teaching gifts and service gifts. Let's use that perspective as we move forward.

*"As each has received a gift, use it to serve one another, as good stewards of God's varied grace: **Whoever speaks**, as one who speaks oracles of God; **Whoever serves**, as one who serves by the strength that God supplies; so that in everything God may be glorified through Jesus Christ."* 1Peter 4:10-11

TEACHING GIFTS

Heavy emphasis is always placed on the teaching ministry of the church. Service gifts are important in maintaining the church, but when you consider that it is only sound doctrine that saves someone from Hell (1Timothy 4:15 and 2Timothy 3:15) and it is sound doctrine that matures believers, it becomes very obvious that teaching gifts grow the church both numerically and spiritually. A miracle or a healing cannot save anyone or mature anyone.

Recall that the Corinthians had every gift imaginable, but they were the most immature group of believers Paul ever had to deal with, along with the Galatians. The miraculous may point to the truth, but the truth must be articulated in a known human language whether written, spoken, or signed, and in an intelligible fashion so a lost person can comprehend his or her need for Christ, and so an immature believer can grow in the grace and knowledge of Jesus Christ. This process of intelligently conveying the truth in a loving way is purely by God's design.

⌘

"And He gave some as apostles, and some as prophets, and some as evangelists, and some as pastors and teachers, for the equipping of the saints for the work of service, to the building up of the body of Christ..." Ephesians 4:11-12

⌘

Apostles. The Apostle Paul simply listed these men as gifts to the church. As mentioned before, it is obvious we no longer have genuine apostles of Christ who are handpicked by Jesus and who can work the "signs of an apostle." We have to acknowledge the apostolic gift to the church is the foundational role they played as noted in Ephesians 2:20, where we have *"been built on the foundation of the apostles and prophets, Christ Jesus Himself being the corner stone."*

As long as the Church exists we will enjoy the fruit of their first century labor of cementing all of our doctrines into what we call the New Testament. True, there were other men labeled as apostles of the church, but their calling was more general. These men included Barnabas, Silas, James, the Lord's brother, Epaphroditus, and a few other brethren. But only the original Twelve (with Paul replacing Judas) were ever called the apostles of Christ, and they will have their names inscribed on the 12 foundation stones within the New Jerusalem (Revelation 21:14).

Some might ask about the validity of Paul being the twelfth apostle, and how would Mathias fit into the picture since he was selected by the other eleven apostles to replace

Judas. The key requirement for an apostle was to be handpicked by Jesus, Himself. The book of Acts clearly describes Paul's unique calling by Christ in that regard.

Scripture also gives us precedence of God replacing key people within a defined group. For example, if you look at the listed names of the twelve tribes in Revelation 7 they are different from those listed in Genesis 49. The tribe of Dan is missing, and Manesseh, who was one of the two sons of Joseph, is inserted in Dan's place. We can only speculate why that is so. Some say because Dan was steep in idolatry (Judges 18:30); or possibly due to a Jewish tradition that the antichrist was to come from the tribe of Dan. We can conclude that the apostles of Christ are, likewise, fixed for all eternity. Their gift to the church is one of a kind. All we can do is to continue to build on their foundation.

Prophets and Prophecies. Prophets are grouped along with apostles in Ephesians 2:20 as being part of the church's foundation. Cessationists believe the office of prophets have ceased along with the apostles. Therefore, revelatory prophecies and the gift of prophecy have ceased.

Continuationists, on the other hand, believe prophets still exists, but they concede that Scripture is closed, and revelatory prophecies are now of a different caliber. A proponent of the Pentecostal 3rd Wave viewpoint, Dr. C. Samuel Storms, says, in essence, modern-day prophecies can even contain error, and the gift of prophecy does not guarantee the infallible transmission of [an infallible] revelation.[35]

The arguments for and against modern-day prophets and prophecies are intense with all sides doing their best to convince people that their respective convictions are the right ones. What can the rest of us do to determine which side has the correct doctrine? We can only echo the need to stick with Scripture.

New Testament prophets include Agabus (Acts 11:28), Judas and Silas (Acts 15:32), and the four daughters of Philip the evangelist (Acts 21:8-9). Luke 2:26-38 mentions the prophetess, Anna, but she is seen as an Old Testament prophetess since she was the last prophetic individual to acknowledge and welcome the Messiah into the world. We have no idea what Philip's daughters prophesied about or where they prophesied. Since prophecies were intended for believers (1Corinthians 14) we can assume they prophesied within the church for the benefit of believers.

Agabus only rendered two prophecies we are aware of. The first one was in regards to a famine which eventually took place in that part of the world (Acts 11:28). The second recorded in Acts 21 foretold that the Apostle Paul would be handed over to the Gentiles – which he was. That's all we know about New Testament prophets and their prophecies.

1Corinthians 14 provides some additional insight into the high value of prophetic utterances. Specifically, in

---

[35]Wayne G. Grudem, general editor. (1996). *Are Miraculous Gifts for Today*. Grand Rapids: Zondervan. 207-209

1Corinthians 14:5, Paul says he desired for the whole church to prophesy. Some take this to mean it is possible for everyone to have the gift of prophecy, but the context seems to elaborate on the church stressing the need to encourage those who have the gift of prophecy to use it for the edification of the church.

Since prophecy was a teaching gift, and teaching has the highest priority in the church (not tongues), this is what Paul tried to stress to this Corinthian church. But to the typical Pentecostal to whom subjective feelings and experiences have priority over sound biblical doctrine, the Bible is just not enough. Something more is always needed to give them the spiritual high they seek.

Therefore, knowing that prophets were part of the foundation of the church in the same way as the apostles, their function was to clearly edify or grow the church through revealing God's truth, as did the apostles. Since the canon of Scripture is closed as acknowledged by the Church at large and especially by intrinsic teachings of Scripture, revelatory prophecies are passé, gone, obsolete, over. We have to logically assume that prophets along with the gift of prophecy and all revelatory prophecies are also no longer with us. Any and all "prophetic utterances" can be done by virtually anyone with the ability to communicate or forth-tell God's truth. The foretelling of new revelations is gone.

Evangelists, Pastors/Teachers. These two offices are still present within the church as acknowledged by everyone in Christendom. There are neither explicit nor implicit teachings in Scripture that allude to their demise over time. Timothy was acknowledged as an evangelist, and he was encouraged by Paul to pass on specific knowledge to other faithful men (1Timothy 2:2), who in turn would pass it on to others. Plus, Timothy and Titus were both charged by Paul to select qualified men who can stand up to be church elders. The elders constituted the pastors who also had the ability to teach within the church.

Someone did not automatically become an evangelist or a pastor/teacher at the moment of salvation. They had to grow in that position, and be tested over time. In fact, if someone were to say, "Hey, I've got the gift of pastoring," a church would be foolish to put them in a shepherding position without first being grounded in the word of God and after being tested for faithfulness and maturity. Even deacons were to be first tested (1Timothy 3:10) before entering that special office. Paul acknowledged in 1Timothy 5:17 that *"The elders who rule well are to be considered worthy of double honor, especially those who work hard at preaching and teaching."* This passage clearly reflects the priority of teaching within the church.

Other Teaching Gifts – Wisdom and Knowledge. Wisdom and knowledge are often considered part of the so-called sign gifts, which also include tongues, the interpretation of tongues, faith, prophecy, healings and miracles. I group these two gifts of wisdom and knowledge together because I agree with Pentecostal theologian, Gordon Fee, that the difference between Wisdom and Knowledge "is perhaps forever lost to us."[36] That statement by a leading Pentecostal theologian says volumes about the cessation of

---

[36] Gordon Fee, Empowering Presence (Peabody, Mass.: Hendrickson, 1991, p.167-168.

those two gifts. If we are not able to even define what these gifts are and how they are to work in the church, then there is no way we can prove who has got which gift and if they are even being used properly.

One gross misapplication of these two gifts often seen and heard frequently in Pentecostal-type churches is when someone with a so-called word of wisdom or knowledge publicly reveals someone's sin to the congregation – "I know what you did last summer." First of all, revealing someone's sin in a public forum violates the Matthew 18 principle where it basically states if someone has something against a brother, it needs to be dealt with privately before it is elevated to a larger audience for resolution.

Some may argue that the gifts of wisdom and knowledge help fulfill 1Corinthians 14:24-25 where it states *"But if all prophesy, and an unbeliever or an ungifted man enters, he is convicted by all, he is called to account by all; the secrets of his heart are disclosed; and so he will fall on his face and worship God, declaring that God is certainly among you."* First of all, it is the prophesying or the revealing of God's truth that brings conviction to a person's heart, and not the revealing of that person's sin.

Even if a person does receive some kind of truthful revelation about another person (just like the damsel in Acts 16:16 who received successful stock tips for her masters to reap gains) does not mean such revelation came from God. From a cessationist viewpoint, since the word of wisdom and word of knowledge have ceased, such modern revelation of wisdom or knowledge is definitely not from God.

One time, my wife, Karen, a registered nurse, was asked to help out on the psychiatric ward of her hospital where all the psychotic, schizophrenic, and other mentally impaired patients are treated. This was an unusual request since she is a labor and delivery nurse, but they needed extra help since they were understaffed and over worked in that ward on that particular day. She got her patient assignment and she entered the room to introduce herself to the patient but noticed that the patient and some family members were talking on the other side of the curtain. Not wanting to interfere with the family discussions she stayed on the opposite side of the curtain waiting for them to wrap up. With the curtain separating them, the family didn't even perceive Karen had entered the room, and Karen, herself, was unable to see who was on the other side of the curtain. Yet, the patient said to the family members, "You must all go now, because I need to talk with my nurse, Karen." No other nurse had the name of Karen who had previously been tending this patient. Are demonic forces still at work today, and can they surreptitiously reveal tidbits of information to humans in the so-called words of wisdom and knowledge? According to Scripture, yes they can.

Other Teaching Gifts – Tongues and Interpretation of Tongues. Tongues and the interpretation of tongues were to work together. They were not designed to work separately, unless, as we see in Acts 2 and Acts 11, the listeners were multi-lingual so an interpreter wasn't needed. It is amazing how the gift of tongues, which according to Paul is the least of the gifts, causes the most problems in the church today and back in the first century as well. But, once we consider Satan's tricks and devices, it makes perfect sense.

The Corinthians were immature believers, as noted by Paul, so Satan took the least of the gifts and made it a preeminent gift to them. The gift of tongues is addressed only in Mark, Acts and 1Corinthians. All total, the gift of tongues is mentioned in 30 verses scattered within 3 books, 7 chapters, of which 17 verses (~60%) are used to correct its misuse.

Christians are not the only ones able to speak in unknown tongues. Mormons, Muslims, Buddhists, witch doctors, Satanists, Tibetan monks, and even some mentally ill patients speak in tongues. John MacArthur, in his book *Charismatic Chaos*, cites that reports have come from East Africa telling of persons possessed by demons who speak fluently in Swahili or English, languages they have never learned. Among the Thonga people of Africa, when a demon is exorcised, a song is usually sung in Zulu even though the Thonga people do not know Zulu. The one doing the exorcising is supposedly able to speak Zulu by a miracle of tongues.[37]

W. A. Criswell (1909 - 2002), a one-time pastor of my home church in Mount Washington, Kentucky, and described as one of the 20th century's greatest expository preachers and the patriarch of the "Conservative Resurgence" within the Southern Baptist Convention[38] had this to say about tongues: "In the long story of the church, after the days of the apostles,

[37]John F. MacArthur, J. (1992). Charismatic Chaos. Grand Rapids: Zondervan Publishing House. 292.

[38]http://en.wikipedia.org/wiki/W._A._Criswell.

wherever the phenomenon of glossolalia has appeared it has been looked upon as heresy....[and] it has never been accepted by the historical churches of Christendom. It has been universally repudiated by these churches as a doctrinal and emotional aberration."[39]

The one critical factor the early church's tongue speaking had over all others was the INTELLIGENCE FACTOR. True tongues speaking were of known human languages as indicated in Acts 2:11 and 11:16. Nowhere does Scripture teach that the gift of tongues was anything other than a known intelligible human language. Luke even recalls Peter's words that the "*Holy Spirit fell upon them just as He did upon us at the beginning*" (Acts 11:16). Remember, we can only prove things according to Scripture, and these passages are the only passages depicting tongues in actual use. This becomes our gauge to go by. The gift of tongues had a definite purpose: 1) to confirm the apostle's authority was from God; 2) to show the inclusion of Gentile people groups; and 3) to be a sign of judgment on Israel.

John MacArthur recited how William Samarin, professor of linguistics at the University of Toronto, described modern-day "glossolalia." After traveling the world over investigating the practice of tongues from the snake handlers of the Appalachia to Russia and to third world countries, he summed up his study by stating, "Yet in spite of similarities, glossolalia is fundamentally not language." MacArthur went

[39]W. A. Criswell, "Facts Concerning Modern Glossolalia," in *The Holy spirit in Today's Church,* ed. Erling Jornstad (Nashville: Abingdon, 1973), 90-91.

further to state that all the many studies on glossolalia agree that what we are hearing today is not language; and if it is not language, then it is not of the biblical gift of tongues.[40]

While attending an early morning Bible study at work one time, which was led by a Pentecostal pastor, one of our discussions centered on the gift of tongues. I asked him to explain how he justified that tongues were unintelligible gibberish when Acts 2 depicts tongues as known human languages. After circling the various Scripture passages on the topic, he said he suddenly received a revelation from the Holy Spirit that the miracle in Acts 2 weren't the apostles speaking in tongues, but the miracle was in the unsaved listeners hearing the Gospel in their respective home languages. Such self-validating experiences are all too common within Pentecostal/Charismatic circles. No matter how accurate I could articulate the Scriptures on this topic his new revelation, supposedly from the Holy Spirit, prevailed over any further logical and reasonable discussions on the matter. And he couldn't tell me how he knew it was the Holy Spirit who gave him that revelation except to say he just knew from experience it was the Holy Spirit.

Biblical tongues had a definite and finite purpose – to convey God's message to unbelievers and to edify others when interpreted. It was not meant to be your personal prayer language or just to be a show-off gift as you rambled off unintelligible gibberish. Tongues as an individual prayer language were outside the scope of its true purpose, and the

[40]John F. MacArthur, J. (1992). *Charismatic Chaos.* Grand Rapids: Zondervan Publishing House. 278.

only function praying in tongues served was to boost the ego of the one praying, and this was not conveyed by Paul in a positive manner, but in a derogatory manner.

This ego-boosting aspect of privately praying in tongues was not what Paul was encouraging. But Pentecostals put a positive spin on privately praying in tongues to make it sound plausible and biblical. According to 1Corinthians 14:19, intelligent speaking has priority and is critical to the life and growth of a church. When showmanship gifts have priority over edification gifts, problems loom.

John MacArthur gave a succinct answer why tongues have exploded with such force within Christendom. "Many are seeking an alternative to the cold, lifeless Christianity that permeates so many churches. People who join the Pentecostal/Charismatic movement often are those who are looking for action, excitement, warmth, and love. They want to believe that God is really at work in their lives – right her and now."[41]

Just when you think you have heard it all, someone comes up with a new twist on things. One Pentecostal-leaning preacher on TV was explaining his heavenly language and how all tongues speaking is in the heavenly language. Nothing new there, but he went on to explain how he received revelation for the origination of man speaking God's heavenly language. He went on to explain that prior to the Tower of Babel man was in "one accord" and everyone spoke with a single tongue or language, the heavenly language.

---

[41]John F. MacArthur, J. (1992). *Charismatic Chaos.* Grand Rapids: Zondervan Publishing House. 298.

Only after the Tower of Babel were other languages introduced. Then at Pentecost when the disciples were gathered in "one accord" they spoke in tongues, or actually, spoke once again using the heavenly language. The truly sad part of this story is that studio camera pan shots of the audience showed some nodding in agreement with this preacher. Where is their discernment? As B. B. Warfield said so accurately when it comes to chasing the miraculous, Christians "no longer knew how to distinguish between truth and falsehood."[42]

I also question the preacher's hermeneutics more than anything. Playing word games, especially between Hebrew and Greek, can lead to anything a person wants it to lead to. This preacher basically injected his doctrine into the passages (eisegesis or inference) instead of extracting his doctrine from the passages (exegesis).

Pentecostal minister Gordon Fee made the statement, "There is simply no way to know if tongues-speaking is the same in kind as in Acts."[43] With this proclamation from a respected Pentecostal representative, how can Pentecostals continue putting modern tongues on par with those identified in Scripture? Tongues, like prophecies, were never meant to be chaotic or unintelligible.

---

[42]Warfield, B. B. (Originally Published 1918, Republished 2012). *Counterfeit Miracles.* New York: Charles Scribner's Sons (1918) and Forgotten Books (2012). 74.

[43]Gordon Fee, Author, Christian theologian, & AIG minister, *Empowering Presence, p.890.*

Tongues and the interpretation of tongues were tied together. One should not be without the other to convey God's prophetic truth and edify the body. Even prophecies had to be tested for validity. Therefore tongues were to be tested for truth and accuracy after they were interpreted by an interpreter.

Here is the toughest issue when it comes to tongues speaking. According to 1Corinthians 14:34, women are to be silent in the church. When you consider the context (chapters 12, 13 and 14 are actually one paragraph in the Greek), it is hard to escape that women were to keep silent in regards to speaking in tongues. We see from other passages in Scripture that it was appropriate for women to talk, pray and prophesy in church (1Corinthians 11:5; Acts 2:17; 21:9; Luke 2:36-38 – the prophetess Anna spoke in the temple). Why was it improper or shameful for women to speak in tongues in church? Once again we can only speculate since we do not have enough information to formulate a hard fast dogmatic doctrine.

By Pentecostals' own admission, who does most of the tongues speaking in their churches? Women! Pentecostals have fallen into a subtle devise of Satan, and they refuse to admit it that they are in violation of a clear command in Scripture. Of course, the answer they put forward to resolve this dilemma of violating God's word is 14:34, which, they interpret, depicts a cultural issue in the Corinthian church.

Most theologians agree that women having to wear a head covering was definitely a cultural issue as born out in 1Corinthians 11:3-16, but a cultural issue is not alluded to in 1Corinthians 14:34 where it plainly states, *"The women are to keep silent in the churches; for they are not permitted to speak, but are to subject themselves, just as the Law also says."*

Paul stated in 1Corinthians 14:39. '*...forbid not to speak with tongues.*' Tongues were still in existence then, so that was an appropriate command. Today, we need to show from scripture the "*more excellent* way" – how to live by faith and love, not by sight and sound. Romans 1:11 depicts that the bestowing of a spiritual gift establishes one in the faith. This "spiritual gift" is sound doctrine according Paul's statements in Romans 16:25-26 and Colossians 2:7.

Some may ask, "Well, what about those rare situations where some missionaries have testified of sharing their faith to an unbeliever of a different nationality and a different language, with neither party having learned the language of the other?" Those do seem to be rare and unique events, if they happened as told. Since they are not able to repeat the event at will, it cannot be considered a spiritual gift. Even the missionary does not realize they had been speaking in a different language until someone says to them, "I didn't know you spoke that language" and the missionary responds, "I don't." Again, such stories are always 2nd and 3rd hand and cannot be verified.

Such events are not the norm for us to bank on. If we give too much credence to these rare events, which occur outside of Scripture, they could distract us and even be a snare to some. Gideon found this out when he made an ephod, which was a priestly garment associated with the ability to receive communication from God. This particular ephod became an object of idolatrous worship for his family and all of Israel instead of God (Judges 8:27). We have to be careful of converting unverified stories into reliable affirmation of doctrine. We could be chasing whatever itches our ear (2Timothy 4:3).

SERVICE GIFTS

The various service gifts within the church are identified as those which help promote meeting the physical and emotional needs within the body of Christ. These include grace and faith (which are bestowed in some capacity upon every believer). Other service gifts include ministry, giving, rules or management, mercy, gifts of healings, miracles, discernment, helps, and administration.

It is amazing how God seems to over gift some people with extraordinary talents and others are challenged even to be able to walk and talk at the same time. My oldest daughter is quite gifted in some areas. She is artistically and musically inclined. One day the movie *Chariots of Fire* came on television, and when the musical score was played, my daughter, who refused to sit still long enough to take piano lessons, said "Hey, I can play that." Sure enough, she went over to the piano and banged it out as pretty as anything, but for her to discipline herself to take lessons was near impossible. Her mother and I eventually gave up with that fruitless endeavor. Her younger sister, on the other hand, is artistically and musically challenged. She has trouble drawing stick figures, and she had to toil long and hard just to play chopsticks on the piano. But she persevered with her piano lessons, and today, she is quite accomplished in the musical arena.

A gift, then, is something one receives either at birth or, as some believe, as a result of God endowing them with some capability at the moment of salvation. Some Pentecostals believe that additional gifts can be received from God at subsequent refillings of the Holy Spirit. In contrast, a talent can be defined as something developed over time, such as woodworking, teaching, computer programming, driving, preaching, and even parenting.

As noted previously how do we tell if someone has the gift of mercy or is just being merciful? How do we tell if someone has the gift of giving or is simply following the principles to give? How do we tell if someone has the gift of helps, hospitality, administration, or ministry from those who have stepped up to the plate to do what is needed to get things done? Since such gifts are quite subjective, there is no way to tell.

We can see in many people, especially after they mature in their faith, specific leanings, strengths, and talents which have developed over time – and we call those people gifted in those areas. But to be able to tell what gift a person receives at the moment of salvation is impossible in our day and age. When a Pentecostal proclaims they received the gift of tongues at the moment of salvation, which is the least of all the gifts, they are not able to confirm what other more significant gifts they might have receive as well. We can conclude this gifting of the least of the gifts is out of kilter with Scripture and God's intent for His church, and therefore cannot be from God.

During the first century, however, the immediate gifting of believers with new abilities was apparent. There were not enough elders to guide a young church into maturity, so it looks like God had to instantly equip people to serve in various capacities in His newly-founded churches. Their gifts were apparently given to them in full maturity. They did not have to learn how to discern, teach, rule, administrate, speak in tongues, interpret tongues, heal, or work miracles.

Today, many can buy books, tapes, and DVDs on how to speak in tongues. What is strange is that no one has a book, tape, or a DVD that can be bought to show how to interpret tongues of a so-called heavenly language. Shouldn't they be of the same caliber?

What can be derived from Scripture is that the gifts of the Holy Spirit for today have to be viewed as "talents" that people grow into overtime and not something received at salvation. For example, the gifts of nursery worker, or Sunday School teacher, or even Pastor are not something people are selected for the moment they get saved. Like a deacon, they should first be proven trustworthy and mature.

God has the ultimate responsibility to uniquely position people for ministry in each of His churches throughout the world, and what we have to realize about God's process is EVERYONE IS REPLACEABLE.

Sign Gifts. Here are a few more considerations on the gifts which are often labeled as the sign gifts. The sign gifts listed in the following table with their spontaneous quality were given to believers fully functional and ready for immediate use – and at the full control of the believer. No one had to learn how to speak in tongues, or how to interpret tongues, or how to heal, or how to work a miracle.

If any gifts are controversial today as far as whether or not God has seen fit to continue or cease their functions, it is these sign gifts. We have already talked about wisdom, knowledge, prophecy, tongues and interpretation of tongues. Let us proceed identifying some challenges churches have with the gift of faith, the gifts of healings, and the gift of miracles.

Passage	Individual Sign Gifts	Category
1Corinthians 12:8-10	Wisdom	Teaching
	Knowledge	Teaching
	Faith	Service
	Gifts of Healings	Service
	Miracles	Service
	Prophecy	Teaching
	Tongues	Teaching
	Interpretation of Tongues	Teaching

Gift of Faith. This gift, like the gifts of grace or mercy is not fully defined. Yet, each believer has received a measure of faith (Romans 12:3), and even if someone's faith is smaller than a mustard seed it can be exercised like a muscle to get it to a point where it can achieve great results for the kingdom of God (Matthew 17:20). What is the difference, then, between the faith that each believer possesses with those having the gift of faith; and how do we prove that someone is appropriately exercising the gift of faith for the church? Can they work more miracles than the ones with the gift of miracles? Does the gift of faith go to the ones with the gift of miracles or is it a standalone gift? Again, we cannot tell. We can only speculate.

The first century believers had no problems discerning who had it and how it was to be used. Which means by default for us today, it is a gift that the Holy Spirit has stopped giving to the church – or, it is to be taken as a general gift. That means if someone is using his God-given faith to live a godly life, to remain faithful and fruitful and victorious for the kingdom, then that is as far as we should take it.

Gifts of Healings. This is the only gift which is plural. It is not the gift of healings, where one person can heal every ailment type, but gifts of healings, where presumably, multiple people in a church had the ability to heal any and every ailment. Or, where each gifted person can only heal specific types of ailments. If this was the case, then for the whole church body to be edified, all the gifts of healings would need to be present within each and every church.

It is unknown how the gifts of healings were or would be divided up. Was it alphabetical – abdominal illnesses to Zieve's syndrome? Was it anatomical? For example, some would heal ailments of the head while others could heal body parts such as the torso, limbs, blood, bone, skin, muscle, or specific to male, female, child, or adult. Was it by severity – where some could heal only itchy mosquito bites while others could perform resurrections?

It seems reasonable and plausible that if Jesus could heal 100% of the people 100% of time then so should those with the gifts of healings – but they can't, and they haven't. Cessationists seem to have the stronger position believing that gifts of healings have ceased as well, per the will of God.

Gift of Miracles. Once again, we have to speculate what this gift could do. If someone could work miracles at will could they also heal sicknesses and perform resurrections? Then why have the gifts of healings? If someone with the gift of miracles could at will walk on water, divide the waters, call down fire from heaven as Elijah did, make iron float as Elisha did, physically move mountains and pluck trees out of the ground with just a thought, and a host of other wonders, then who are they and where are they today? Again, cessationists have the stronger position with believing such wonders will not be seen again until the two witnesses appear on the world scene as depicted in Revelation 11.

A Few More Considerations. Pentecostals often throw up the argument that God is the same yesterday, today and forever to help substantiate their claim that whatever Jesus did in the first century can still occur today. But that argument doesn't even stand up to what they preach from the pulpit.

An apostle of Christ was always present when the Holy Spirit was given to a group of people. In Acts 2:3-6, the apostles were present when cloven tongues of fire and intelligible tongues were given to them. In Acts 9:10-17, Paul was present when Ananias of Damascus, a disciple of the Lord, gave Paul the Holy Spirit (with no evidence of tongues). In Acts 8:5-17 Philip in Samaria worked "miracles and signs," but the apostles had to come down to give the Holy Spirit to the Samaritans through the laying on of their hands, and with no evidence of tongues. In Acts 10:16, Peter was present when Cornelius and his Gentile family received the Holy Spirit and the ability to speak in tongues. Finally, in Acts 19:6, Paul laid his hands on the believers in Ephesus to bestow the Holy Spirit and they spoke with tongues and prophesied.

If God is the same today as He was yesteryear, then it should be evident that only a true apostle of Christ can bestow the Holy Spirit on anyone, and not a disciple or other fine Christian. For Pentecostals to differ on this voids their argument that God is the same today, yesterday and forever. Yes, character-wise, He is the same, but God does change His ways, His blessings and compassions, and His gifts at specific junctures throughout the ages.

If Wisdom, Knowledge, Faith, Prophecy, Tongues and Interpretation of Tongues still exist, it is conceivable new revelation can be revealed, which means the Word of God can continue to grow. However, since the Word of God is now static (no longer dynamically growing) as acknowledged by most Christian churches, including Pentecostal churches, there is no reason for these sign gifts to exist. When Pentecostals claim that new revelation is no longer a feature of the sign gifts, then they are acknowledging that God has changed His ways since Acts was written.

DREAMS AND VISIONS

Many Pentecostals believe God can still give revelatory dreams and visions to His people. There is actually a lucrative cottage industry on dream interpretations with over 6,000 books in print. Even on this, we need to factor in several biblical considerations. God did give men and women dreams whereby they could foretell God's directives, even for some heathens. In Genesis 20:3-6, God came to Abimelech in a dream of the night, and said to him, "*Behold, you are a dead man."* And in Judges 7:13 Gideon overheard a non-Jew relating a dream to his friend, and by it, Gideon won a military victory. In Matthew 27:19, while Pilate was sitting on the judgment seat, his wife sent him a message, saying, "*Have nothing to do with that righteous Man (called Jesus) for last night I suffered greatly in a dream because of Him.*"

Revelatory dreams, however, were never common place. God told the Israelites in Numbers 12:6, "*I reveal myself to My prophet in visions, I speak to him in dreams*"; and in Job 33:14-17, *"For God does speak ...in a dream, in a vision of the night...(that) he may speak in men's ears and terrify them with warnings"* (NIV).

God also gave clear warnings against dreams. In Zechariah 10:2 *"... the diviners see lying visions and tell false dreams; they comfort in vain. Therefore the people wander like sheep."* In Jeremiah 29:8, *"...and God said to Israel "Do not listen to the dreams which [your prophets] dream."* Also in 23:32, "*Behold, I am against those who have prophesied false dreams,*" declares the LORD, "*and related them and led My people astray.*"

While in my undergraduate studies, I was struggling to maintain a "B" in Calculus II. One calculus problem kept me busy for more than two days trying to figure out the answer. Finally, I resolved to call it quits, call it a night, and take a "C" for may grade. But around 2:00 in the morning I woke up after dreaming about the problem and the answer was obvious to me. I got up out of bed, went to my study, wrote down the answer, went back to bed, and turned my homework in the following day. To my delight, the answer that came to me while dreaming about the calculus problem the night before was correct. Does that make my dreams worth listening to for direction in life? Not in the least. Such dreams are rare. Solomon says, in essence, we need to place our trust in God's unshakeable word, and not in our dreams (Ecclesiastes 5:7).

More Warnings on Dreams and Visions. But what about Joel 2:28, which Luke quotes in Acts 2:17? "*It will come about after this that I will pour out My Spirit on all mankind; and your sons and daughters will prophesy, Your old men will dream dreams, Your young men will see visions*?"

Cessationists see this fulfilled in Agabus, Barnabas, Simeon, Lucius, Manaen, Paul, and the four daughters of Philip (Acts 11:28; 13:1-2; 16:9-10; 21:9-10). A biblical principle on dreams is to trust in God's objective word and not in subjective dreams. People receive their dreams while not in full control of their faculties and possibly under more of the influence of something eaten the night before, or the pressures of the previous day. Colossians 2:18 warns us "*not to be fooled by those who take a stand on their visions and dreams*."

Tom Doyle, an evangelist and pastor, wrote a book called *Dreams and Visions*,[44] in which he records a series of real stories from Muslims who follow Christ and who did so because they had a dream about Jesus. He adds that the phenomenon is taking place in Saudi Arabia, Iran, Egypt, Syria and on the West Bank. Though their dreams of Jesus do not save the Muslims, according to Doyle, they become a starting point to find a Bible, or find a Christian, and ask what these dreams mean. Doyle even claims ninety-five percent of

[44] Tom Doyle and Greg Webster, *Dreams and Visions*, (Tomas Nelson, 2012)

the Muslims who are now Jesus followers say that they were led to Christ by someone explaining the dream to them.[45]

Are such dreams, as Doyle purports, in line with Scripture? We can only point to Cornelius in Acts 10 where he received a dream to chase down the Apostle Peter who then would preach the Gospel to him. God always uses a human agent to preach the Gospel to the lost with only one exception – when, during the final days of man's tenure on the earth, He uses an angel to preach the "eternal gospel" to those remaining (Revelation 14:6).

Are dreams reliable and can dreams motivate or confirm for us any decisions we need to make? Dreams may be of God as noted in Joel 2:28; or they may be "lying" dreams as seen in Zechariah 10:2; or they can be a result from physical weariness as Solomon tells us in Ecclesiastes 5:3. In Ecclesiastes 5:7, Solomon says we are to fear God and not to trust dreams, and Jeremiah 23:28 says that God holds His word above man's dreams. We should take Paul's teaching serious about proving all things before we take hold of it as truth (1Thessalonians 5:21).

Joseph, the earthly father of Jesus, received three dreams from God. The first had him take Mary as his wife (Matthew 1:20). The second dream revealed to him the need to flee to Egypt (Matthew 2:13). And the third dream (Matthew 2:22) had him return to Israel so that Scripture could be fulfilled for the Messiah to come out of Egypt. None of these dreams were

---

[45]http://www.beliefnet.com/columnists/watchwomanonthewall/2013/02/jesus-appears-to-muslims-in-dreams-conversions-and-testimonies-video.html

subjective. Joseph had undeniable directions from God what to do, where to go, and when to act as he was responsible for the Messiah's safety and upbringing.

Our dreams, in contrast, are totally subjective. Also note that God-invoked dreams along with accurate dream interpretations are extremely rare, even in the Bible – so don't use dreams to help make decisions. Trust in known teachings, principles, and revelations found in the Bible.

Jay Adams, in his book, *How to Help People Change,* records the following statement made by the head of an evangelical student movement in a conference held in Austria some years back: "Whenever I don't have time to study my Bible to find the answer to a question, I just ask God to give me the answer in a dream." [46]

Adams went on to voice his concern that the greatest difficulty believers have to face is with people turning to substitutes for the Scriptures, such as putting out fleeces or following some prompting of the Spirit until they get the answers they desire. All this subjective leading boils down to making decisions based on their feelings and not on the objective teachings found within God's established word. We should heed Paul's warning to the "foolish" Galatians and avoid turning to the "weak and beggarly elements" (including subjective dreams) that leads back to bondage (Galatians 4:9).

---

[46] Jay E. Adams, *How to Help People Change,* (Zondervan, 1986), 201

CHAPTER 6
DEMONIC POSSESSION AND DELIVERANCE

And the devil said to [Jesus], "I will give You all this domain and its glory; for it has been handed over to me, and I give it to whomever I wish." Luke 4:6

DEMONS ARE REAL

We, in America, often have blinders on as to what havoc Satan and his horde of miscreants are doing around us, our nation, and throughout the world. According to Scripture they can oppress, obsess, and possess individuals; they can impact a nation's economy and well-being; and as we can see just from the book of Job, Satan can acquire permission from God to control weather phenomena, war, diseases, and life and death.

Since our modern society has migrated away from a Bible-based influence and adopted more of a materialistic world view, most citizens now believe that all economic, political, social, education, health care, and military woes can be resolved with more money, technology, education, or more time. When, in fact, all of our challenges in life are more spiritual in nature. Fortunately, God has given the knowledge, the insight, and the offensive and defensive weapons to win the battles without breaking any laws of nature. That is how powerful His word is.

Discern the Spirits. One of the pressing biblical truths is that spiritual warfare is a reality, and it is a priority for us to deal with – and we have been losing that war for a very long time. Just from an American perspective, we can see casualties from this costly battle. Just 30 years ago there were only

250,000 people in prisons throughout America. Today, there are more than 2,500,000 people in U.S. prisons.

Another horrendous statistic is the number of abortions in our land – over 56 million since the landmark Roe v Wade verdict in 1973, and still climbing at more than 1,000 each day. That is a lot of future tax payers being flushed down the drain, literally. Worldwide, abortions exceed by best estimates more than 1.3 billion. That is approaching 20% of the world's 7 billion occupants. We are destroying our future by killing off future doctors, nurses, teachers, Nobel prize winners, explorers, business leaders, and discoverers of new technologies and new cures for many of man's pressing challenges.

We are not wrestling against flesh and blood, or against the IRS, or even against terrorists, but against the spiritual rulers, against the spiritual powers, against the world forces of this darkness, against the spiritual forces of wickedness in the heavenly places as Ephesians 6:12 says. The sad part is we don't even show up for the war, so we are defeated before we even pick up a weapon to fight it.

Who are these spiritual rulers? The Bible calls them demons, often known as fallen angels. The head of this nefarious army is called Satan, Lucifer, that serpent of old, the Devil, the father of all lies, the dragon, the god of this world, and the prince of the power of the air, just to list a few of his names. Their mission, since they cannot fight and win against God, is to do everything they can to hurt, afflict, destroy, and even kill the epitome of God's creation – mankind. When Satan received permission from God to afflict Job, but not to kill him, Satan did the next best thing. He afflicted Job so bad

Job wished he were dead. Satan killed Job's ten children, and destroyed his wealth and health.

But why? Consider this: God did not make any of His created beings to be robots without a free will to choose. Instead, He created all of us and all of His angels to have a meaningful existence. God would love to see every one of His beloved creatures (angels and men) to willingly and wholeheartedly choose to be with Him. But Satan, and presumably, a hoard of other angelic beings, opted to go their own way, which was away from God. Since God did not create an alternative universe outside of His reach, there is only one final destiny for Satan and his cohorts in crime, and that is Hell (Matthew 25:41). Unfortunately, though Hell was made for the Devil and his angels, it will also be the final abode of all unrepentant men and women, who, like Satan, willfully choose not to be with God.

God is such a just God, a righteous God, even a fair God, that before He casts Satan and His angels into Hell He allows Satan and his minions every opportunity (within limits, of course) to defeat Him and His plan for mankind; hence, the turmoil we see on individual levels, national levels, and on a global level. It is not that man would not be just as evil and diabolical without the influences of the Prince of Darkness, but satanic and demonic influences do add a different dimension to our existence here on earth.

The Solution! But what about us, the epitome of God's creation who are at a distinct disadvantage since we cannot directly see into the angelic or demonic worlds? It looks like the only weapon we have at our disposal is a bunch of words in a book called the Bible. But words alone do nothing. There must be a power source behind those words.

That is where God comes in, along with His indwelling Holy Spirit and the redemptive work of Jesus Christ. In brief, God chooses to work in our lives for our good when we are willingly obedient to His commands, principles, and directives found in the Bible. We can find guidance to resolve all of our challenges in life at the individual level, the national level, and even on the global level. We just need to willingly read and heed His word to reap His blessings He so freely wants to give to us on a daily basis.

All those words above are nice at the 40,000 foot level, but what about at the street level? How do we contend with evil that resides in us and around us, and implement what we find in Scripture at the individual level? We must realize that what we do at the individual or "grass roots" level bubbles up to the national and global levels.

People struggle with addictions (drugs, pornography), with emotions (anger, hate), with handicaps (physical, mental, social), and with finances (not enough income, too much debt). Where is God's solution in all this? Remember we are not put into a position that God cannot get us out of. Every challenge we will ever experience is common to man. As seen in 1Corinthians 10:13, "*No temptation has overtaken you but such as is common to man; and God is faithful, who will not allow you to be tempted beyond what you are able, but with the temptation will provide the way of escape also, so that you will be able to endure it.*"

Nothing has ever taken God by surprise. He knows our every need even before we ask Him, our every thought before we think it, and our every sin before we commit it.

Scott Stuart and Heath Lambert, in their book *Counseling the Hard Cases,*[47] demonstrate how people saddled with debilitating social, physiological, and psychological conditions as a result of sexual abuse, obsessive compulsive disorders (OCD), postpartum depression, paralyzing fears, anorexia, bipolar disorders, homosexuality, chemical addictions, adultery, dissociative identity disorders (DID), or multiple personalities disorders (MPO) can overcome their ailments along with associated negative social stigmas, through the all sufficiency and authority of Scripture. In each of the cases highlighted in Stuart's book, demons were never exorcised out of anyone. Tormented people received back their mental health, their physical health, and their social health by implementing biblical principles. In essence, any demons in their lives left when God's word was emphatically obeyed.

How the Devil Works. Let's consider some of the hard cases, because once we see the principles of how God can work in the most deplorable of situations they will transpose nicely to the myriads of easier cases.

Most Christians acknowledge we can sin rather easily even without Satan's help, because we do what we want to, we go where we want to go, we say what we want to say, and we think what we want to think. We don't really need Satan's

---

[47]Stuart, S. a. (2012). *Counseling the Hard Cases.* Nashville, TN, USA: B&H Publishing Group.

influence to sin against God because we can do it quite well all by ourselves.

Dr. Robert D. Jones, biblical counseling professor at Southeastern Baptist Theological Seminary in Wake Forest, North Carolina says, "Every counselor should have at least one hard cast – a stubborn, slow to change person – to serve as a perpetual reminder that sin is deep, change is hard, growth is progressive, love requires patience, and God alone transforms people in his time and in his way."[48]

Satanic or demonic influence can play a part in someone's life to wreak havoc on a larger scale. We may not see actual demons at work, but we can realize demonic activity based on the teachings of Scripture. Just reading about the various incidences in the Bible on demons and the damage they can do to someone's health, wealth, and social life gives us insight what they are allowed to do. Fortunately, we can also see from Scripture what they cannot do. If we were to categorize the activities demons invoke into the lives of human beings it would be oppression, obsession, and possession.

Demonic Oppression. The devil knows our weaknesses better than we do ourselves. He knows where to hit us the hardest, and knows how to harass and fight us to make us crumble, and to cause others to stumble as a result of our failure. That is why Paul tells us to be aware of Satan's devices and strategies and for us to put on the whole armor of God, and not just a few pieces, to be able to stand up, fight back, and win those battles.

---

[48]Scott, S. a. (2012). *Counseling the Hard Cases.* Nashville, TN, USA: B&H Publishing Group. 285

The battle begins in the mind, not in the environment, or in someone's lineage. As Scripture says, we are drawn to sin because of our own lusts (James 1:14), our own willingness to do our own thing, to do things our own way, and to be supreme over what we think we have control of, whether it be possessions, positions, or people.

When things do not go our way we often fight, whine, and cry. Then despair sits in, anger sits in, and we begin to drift away from any sensible and reasonable course of actions to fix what is broken in our lives. We often make things worse by striking out at others or internalizing the problem by indulging in some kind of obsession or addiction such as alcohol, drugs, extra-marital affairs, or other forms of self-induced physical and emotional trauma and abuse.

God wants to step in to help us resolve our problems no matter how difficult or complex our problems might be. He often waits till we seek Him, and God has designed the church to be the caretakers of weak and hurting people. Often times a simple and quick solution is all that is required to fix most problems. For example, a thief is commanded to stop stealing and to start working and sharing (Ephesians 4:28).

For some, the command to "go and sin no more" is not easy to implement because of entrenched chemical dependence, physiological complications or even demonic influence. More involvement by God's people who are prepared biblically and spiritually might, then, be needed to break the impasse. Proverbs 20:5 says that *"counsel in a man's heart is deep water; but a man of understanding draws it out."*

Biblical counseling often requires a spiritually mature saint who can thoroughly investigate a situation to help a desperate individual resolve their issues. Unfortunately, many people struggling with various psychological issues, such as psychosis disorders, OCD, and MPO/DID, are labeled as possibly demon-possessed, when in essence sin needs to be dealt with. Dr. Garrett Higbee, clinical psychologist and family counselor says, "The root of all psychological problems are theological errors."[49]

How to Resolve Oppression. The Bible is replete with principles to employ to adequately resolve any and all forms of oppression, whether it is from external sources, internal strife, or even from demonic sources. For people not to avail themselves with the solutions found in the pages of the Bible is nothing short of foolishness. If left unchecked, oppression will eventually lead to obsession with some form of addiction. And as addictions spread to more and more people, then more and more families are destroyed, and eventually a society becomes at risk.

God holds individuals accountable for their sins. Even though Eve was duped by "that serpent of old" in the Garden of Eden she was going to suffer the consequences for willingly doing what God told her and Adam not to do. Likewise, Adam's willingness to go along with his wife and disobey in like fashion had far-reaching repercussions for all of us, which would only be resolved by the redemptive act of the second Adam, Jesus Christ.

---

[49]Scott, S. a. (2012). *Counseling the Hard Cases.* Nashville, TN, USA: B&H Publishing Group. 179.

Until the final closure of history is realized, and Christ sits on His eternal throne, we should be acutely aware of our weaknesses and how Satan can easily exploit them. More important than that, we must be willing to live obediently to God's word, to trust in His guidance, and be willing to confess our sins as soon as they become known. This constitutes living by faith.

When Cain was contemplating doing harm to his brother, Abel, as seen in Genesis 4, God had a unique encounter with Cain. Basically, God had a heart-to-heart meeting with him and asked him "*Why are you angry and why have you got a bad attitude*?" Then God told Cain that "*sin's desire is to master you, but you must master it*" (Genesis 4:6-7).

Unfortunately, Cain did not heed God's warning. Instead, he opted to do his own thing his own way, and he murdered his brother. Cain's problem started in his mind, and he did not take control of it. Instead of following God's word, he followed his emotions.

Here are eight common principles everyone should be fully aware of to avoid becoming oppressed by one's circumstances:

1. We must be willing to forsake our sins: "*Choose this day whom you will serve*" (Joshua 24:15)
2. We must flee temptation and not hang around and toy with it even for one moment (2Timothy 2:22)
3. We must replace bad habits with good habits: e.g., "*Stop stealing, and start working and giving*" (Ephesians 4:28)

4. We must focus or dwell on godly things – those things which are true, honorable, just, right, pure, and good and not on evil things (Philippians 4:8)
5. We must confess our sins to God (1John 1:9) and to others appropriately (James 5:16)
6. We must pursue righteousness (1Timothy 6:11)
7. We should seek help before the roof caves in: "*Call for the elders*" (James 5:14)
8. We must take responsibility and initiate the biblical steps necessary to master the sin in our lives

These eight basic practices are just a part of hiding God's word in our hearts so we do not sin against Him (Psalms 119:11). His "burden" or the responsibilities he asks us to carry are not hard. In fact, living for Christ and doing things God's way is a whole lot easier than doing things our way. God assumes all the pressure when we are obedient to him. This is health to the body and salvation to the soul.

Demonic Obsession – Vexed from Within. If Satan had his way he would have his demons take possession of every soul in the world, and totally consume the place where the Holy Spirit should be residing in each individual. The Holy Spirit, however, does put Satan on a leash with limitations and restrictions. Scripture tells us Satan even has to get permission before he is able to afflict anyone, especially God's chosen believers. Satan got permission to afflict Job, and he also got permission to sift Peter as wheat (Luke 22:31). But before he goes after possessing someone, where he virtually influences their every action, he begins with giving people an obsession.

This obsession can take the form of addictions. We Americans, including Christians, have more addictions than we want to admit. Addictions include spending too much time devoted to the television or the computer, to eating, to playing, to work – and those are some of the easy ones that consume our time and resources in a negative way. Where we should be devoting more time to family relationships, to church, and to God, we prefer to indulge ourselves into more worldly adventures that give us physical and emotional pleasures we seek. After all, we think we deserve it.

The harder addictions would include drugs, alcohol, pornography, gambling, and a host of other vices. People with such hardcore addictions don't often start there, but they begin on a smaller scale. When Dr. James Dobson interviewed serial killer, Ted Bundy, in 1978, who admitted to raping and killing more than 30 women and girls and was suspected of killing more than 50, Bundy said it all began with his obsession with pornography.

How are Obsessions and Addictions Broken? It would be nice if all we had to do was say a simple prayer in the name of Jesus, and presto wham-o, our problems are fixed. Unfortunately, a problem such as a hardcore addiction that took years to develop could take years to resolve with blood, sweat, and tears on all parties involved, because the human will is involved.

We cannot truly help anyone unless they first want help. We can't even help ourselves unless we want to be helped. There is a saying in the counseling world that people won't seek help until they are "sick and tired of being sick and tired."

Many people with addictions simply want more money, or to be left alone, or to be given more time. They do not see the need for or want God to step into their pitiful situation. From a counseling perspective, we must discern between honest and valid requests for help, frivolous wants, controlling and manipulative behavior, and outright scams.

We have the responsibility to be on the lookout to do good to those less fortunate than ourselves. Simply distributing money, for example, to try to fix a bad situation could be the worst thing to do to achieve God's desire for a needy person. To bypass known biblical principles and indiscriminately distribute unearned funds or other forms of help with little, if any, investigation and accountability could do more harm than good to both the recipient and the giver. We have to do our homework as counselors and dig into the underlying problem, which are often spiritual problems. For those of us who have been reconciled to Christ we cannot escape the responsibility God as given to each of us as ministers of reconciliation (2Corinthians 5:18).

First of all, bypassing biblical principles leaves God out of the equation. Giving an addict money, or caving into an angry person's whims might provide a Band-Aid fix but the core problem is still ever present. Plus, we basically enable and encourage a person to continue in his bad behavior, and we actually prolong and perpetuate the misery he might be in, with making other lives miserable. The giver of help would also be short-changed by not reaping a true reward from God for doing things His way.

Tough Love. Sometimes the best course of action for certain situations is to give no help. Why? Some may need to eat out of a pig's trough to learn some valuable lessons from God. If the Prodigal Son, who was addicted to things this sinful world had to offer, had access to the resources of a nearby church, an organization like the Salvation Army, or a gullible giver to keep him from eating with the pigs, he would not have come to his senses and gone back to his family with a humbled spirit as quickly as he did. In fact, it looks like the Prodigal Son came to his senses only after he realized no one would give him anything.

⌘

"And he would have gladly filled his stomach with the pods that the swine were eating, and no one was giving anything to him. But when he came to his senses, he said, 'How many of my father's hired men have more than enough bread, but I am dying here with hunger! I will get up and go to my father, and will say to him, Father, I have sinned against heaven, and in your sight.'"
Luke 15:16-18

⌘

Another reality in our fallen world is God does not often fix "stupid." If someone, even a believer, wants to go off and be stupid – or a prodigal, and squander his money, take on excessive amount of debt, or acquire some hardcore addictions, for the most part, God lets him. The only thing to do is warn, threaten, challenge, and chastise, but sometimes the best thing we can do for the wayward is nothing. Often times they need to learn their lessons through first being humbled much like the Prodigal Son.

In fact, hitting rock bottom is not always a bad thing for Christians or soon-to-be Christians. Sometimes a crisis is needed to make us look up to our Creator from where our true help comes, and force us to remove bad habits and replace them with good ones.

It is sad that some have to have a heart attack or a stroke before improving their diet and exercise so they can enjoy life a while longer. Likewise, it is unfortunate for some to hit skid row, unless God has a unique purpose in it, such as what He accomplished in Job's life. Hitting skid row for some could be a providential opportunity for them to come to their senses and return home humbled and ready to serve the Lord like never before.

Dealing with Addictions. We should never forget our own sinful past when dealing with fallen and hurting people. Some are "enslaved to various lusts and pleasures" and struggle with physical and chemical addictions, which takes direct and guided intervention to bring long-lasting healing to them. Classical life-controlling addictions (passions of the flesh) include sex, drugs, alcohol, and even food.

A Christ-centered approach to consider using to help cure tough sins such as flesh-controlling addictions comes from J. R. Lee and his 12-Step program for addictions called "*Stepping into Freedom.*" Even this program takes discipline for an addict to be willing to make the time and effort to attend sessions and be held accountable. The 12 steps are listed as follows:

1. Admitting Your Powerlessness
2. Acknowledging Your Belief in Jesus Christ
3. Affirming Your Need for God's Care
4. Auditing Your Life ("Examine Yourself")
5. Accounting for Your Actions

6. Agreeing with God
7. Abandoning Your Sins
8. Amending Your Ways
9. Acting on Your Amends
10. Analyzing Your Walk with Christ
11. Anchoring Your Walk with Christ
12. Advancing Your Faith in Christ

Demonic Possession. Demons want to dwell in the human spirit where the Holy Spirit should be. The demon's or demons' purpose is to adversely influence the mind, emotion, and will to do anything but the will of God. There are many incidences in Scripture depicting demon possession.

Matthew 15 gives us a story about a woman desperately seeking a healing for her demon-possessed daughter. She first went directly to the Lord. When He gave her the silent treatment she pursued the other disciples. Because of the woman's persistency the disciples implored Jesus to grant her the request she needed. Jesus, who fully knew the heart of this woman, seemed to have a higher goal in mind to possibly reveal the woman's growing faith in Him.

Jesus ... withdrew into the district of Tyre and Sidon. And a Canaanite woman from that region came out and began to cry out, saying, "Have mercy on me, Lord, Son of David; my daughter is cruelly demon-possessed." But He did not answer her a word. And His disciples came and implored Him, saying, "Send her away, because she keeps shouting at us." But He answered and said, "I

was sent only to the lost sheep of the house of Israel." But she came and began to bow down before Him, saying, "Lord, help me!" And He answered and said, "It is not good to take the children's bread and throw it to the dogs." But she said, "Yes, Lord; but even the dogs feed on the crumbs which fall from their Master's table." Then Jesus said to her, "O woman, your faith is great; it shall be done for you as you wish." And her daughter was healed at once.
Matthew 15:21-28

I get the impression the Lord's silent treatment was His way to dig deeper into her situation and allow her to show her true faith. Barnes' commentary says, "The result shows that it was not unwillingness to aid her, or neglect of her. It was proper that the strength of her faith should be fully tried."

Jesus basically told the woman He was not there to help non-Jews since He was sent to the House of Israel during His earthly ministry. When the woman demonstrated her faith in Him by saying she was just looking for crumbs from the Master's table, Jesus was ready to deliver the help she so desperately was looking for.

When you think about it, this Canaanite woman barged into the Lord's inner sanctum with his disciples who were looking for some much needed down time, and she started badgering them for help. She would not relent. When the Lord basically gave her a NO answer with his refusal to even speak to her, she pursued the disciples till they caved in and tried to persuade Jesus to grant her the help she was persistently asking for. This story is often compared to the parable of the widow who constantly badgered a judge to give her justice and to demonstrate godly persistency in prayer (Luke 18:1-8).

Please note, the Canaanite woman was not looking for a temporary fix for her daughter, but she was looking for a permanent solution to a bad situation that probably impacted her entire family. If this Canaanite woman's faith was not where it should have been and she was just asking for a frivolous request or to somehow scam the Lord out of something, she would have probably walked away empty handed, like those who were anxious for the Lord to work another food miracle (See John 6:26). We might have questioned the Lord's harsh response for giving her the silent treatment since He seemed to have failed to give to someone who asked something of Him, but we always have to remember the higher principle – *"don't cast pearls before swine"* (Matthew 7:6).

In the same fashion, we are not obligated to help everyone who requests help from us, especially if they have unrepentant prodigal behavior. We should, however, diligently investigate the validity of each situation and be ready to render the right kind of help to legitimate needs. This allows the Gospel and the love of Christ to reach the unreachable where they are at.

Since I was raised in a large Catholic family consisting of nine children, I found it interesting that some of my siblings went on to achieve good success in life where they established solid careers, a solid family, and relative peace and tranquility in their careers. On the opposite end of the spectrum, some siblings did not fare so well. They have struggled with finances, addictions, and other social ills. For example, one brother hit skid row and went homeless for more than 20 years. I firmly believe God answered our prayers in how we found him. To make a long story short, a lady befriended my brother when he would visit a McDonald's restaurant to clean up a little after sleeping in a cardboard shack in a vacant lot down the street. Over a few months, this lady gleaned his name and hometown, and through the wonders of the Internet was able to track me down through another brother. I called a cousin in the town he was in who found him in the vacant lot, and within a short period of time we had him medically and mentally examined and placed into an assisted living center where, to this day, he is making progress and adjusting well, but not without challenges all along the way. My brother is diagnosed as manic depressive, and a schizophrenic with multiple personalities disorder (MPO). That is a nice way to say that he has deep and profound issues.

Was Satan directly involved in my brother's situation? What did my brother dabble in to possibly allow one or more demons to torment him? Was it drugs, or pornography, or some other vice? Like me, he accepted Christ in a Pentecostal church. Knowing some of the bizarre behavior that happens in some Pentecostal churches that he was involved in, I even suspected his new found Pentecostal faith had something to do with his mental issues. This story is still unfolding.

A Word of Caution on Deliverance Ministries. With emphases on the spectacular, the miraculous, and even the bizarre, Pentecostals are open to any and all expressions of miraculous works, including demonic activity. According to Dr. Douglas A. Oss, professor of hermeneutics and New

Testament at Central Bible College (Assemblies of God), he acknowledges that signs and wonders within Pentecostal churches are sometimes elevated over truth.[50] Deliverance ministries within these Pentecostal/Charismatic groups, known for exorcising demons out of people, seem to cause more problems than what they solve because of their unbiblical approach to so-called demonic activity.

Bob DeWaay, a Pentecostal pastor, says in his article *How Deliverance Ministries Lead People to Bondage,* that the bondage and deliverance process is very much like a cruel, spiritual "protection racket." "The devil is working both ends of the game like one would in a protection racket. Satan does everything he can to get people into demonic bondage through overt occultism and other means. He then entices Christians who hold to the "warfare" worldview to think that their unbiblical teachings and practices are the key to freedom. Both ends of the game serve Satan's purposes. The devil puts on a convincing show to make it all so very real. He has one of his demons tell the Christian counselor 'secrets' regarding how demons afflict their victims and then leave at the counselor's command."[51]

Jesus claimed that even unsaved Jewish exorcists were able to cast out demons by the power of Satan (Luke 11:19). When it is heard that deliverance ministries take hours and days to cast out demons from people when it took Jesus and the apostles only seconds to cast them out – what are they

---

[50]Wayne G. Grudem, general editor. (1996). *Are Miraculous Gifts for Today.* Grand Rapids: Zondervan. 282.

[51]http://cicministry.org/commentary/issue78.htm.

doing wrong? They might have godly and honorable intentions to help a tormented person, but like the Israelites of old, their zeal for God is not according to knowledge (Romans 10:2). They know neither the Scriptures nor the true power of God (Mark 12:24).

According to Scripture, demonic possession is real, and all explicit and implicit teachings within Scripture do not teach that demonic possession has stopped. So we need to discern the spirits, as we are told in 1John 4:1, and be prepared to help tormented people, especially if they are ready and willing to be helped. Even the demoniacs we find in the pages of the New Testament sought Jesus out.

There are two basic approaches on dealing with demons. The "warfare" approach often taken by deliverance ministries verses the "obedience" approach for lack of a better name. The "warfare" approach addresses the demon, versus the more biblical obedience approach that confronts the person using God's word.

The "warfare" approach uses a quandary of prayers, or what I call, incantations, all said "in Jesus' name," of course, to help win the victory. Sometimes they win, sometimes they don't. Bob DeWaay indicates that Satan will give the Christian warrior a false win. This is where everyone believes the demon is gone, but in actuality the demon is waiting to get back in and do more damage as soon as people meander back to their normal business routines.

Some Christians even claim they have had numerous demons removed from their bodies by exorcist rites, all the while attending various Pentecostal-type churches. To them, all the demonic oppression, obsession, and possession are as real as anything imaginable. From a cessationist's perspective their turmoil could have more easily been resolved, and sooner, and with more permanency through adherence to sound biblical principles and teachings, which comprise the "obedience" approach. The first thing they should have done was to remove themselves from Pentecostal influences.

Whether someone is demon-possessed or not, we have available the same approach to help turn struggling believers and non-believers around positively for the Lord. Paul tells us clearly we are not to be quarrelsome, but be kind to all, able to teach them, patient when wronged, and with gentleness correct those who are struggling. Then, God can do His mighty work to free them from the clutches of the devil, assuming the struggling individual truly wants to be helped.

The Lord's bond-servant must not be quarrelsome, but be kind to all, able to teach, patient when wronged, with gentleness correcting those who are in opposition, if perhaps God may grant them repentance leading to the knowledge of the truth, and they may come to their senses and escape from the snare of the devil, having been held captive by him to do his will. 2 Timothy 2:24-26

THE AUTHORITY OF JESUS AND THE VICTORY OF THE BELIEVER

Demons recognize Jesus' deity and authority, and they have a hatred of Jesus' teaching for they want to be left alone to do the carnage they can with the limited time they have left on this earth. Demons have a cringing fear of Jesus, and of us if we are in God's power through obedient living and being devoted to praying).

Fortunately, demons must always yield to Jesus' authority and not ours. As one demon said to a couple of deliverance ministers – *"Paul I know, and Jesus I know, but who are you?"* And the demon-possessed person proceeded to pounce on the so-called do-gooders, stripped them naked, and sent them running (Acts 19:13-16).

Sin has no hold which cannot be broken through Jesus Christ. Jesus did not tolerate demonic activity. He sent them running out of people within seconds of being in their presence. The demon in the Canaanite's daughter was quickly dispatched with Jesus being miles away from the girl. If Jesus sent the demons scurrying within seconds of confronting a demoniac, and since demon-possession is still with us in our day and age, then we should be prepared to deal with similar situations.

How did the demoniacs get possessed by demons anyway? Scripture actually never says how. It is just a reality that they were. Even a young boy was brought to Jesus with a demon in him (Mark 9:14-29). We could go overboard, as some have, and see a demon in everyone and everything. Some even label every sin as demon-related. The spirit of lust or the spirit of lying is given credit for someone's sin, but it is often times an individual's own lustful spirit that draws him to a sinful lifestyle and not a demonic spirit.

The next question is how do we change those tormented souls who do not want to change? What does it take to convince someone of the error of his ways, such as a drug addict or someone holding onto false doctrines? Again, we can only help those who want help; else we end up casting pearls before swine.

The human will is heavily involved in making change. God told Cain he must master the sin in his life. It is said that someone convinced against their will is of the same opinion still. Even Jesus was not able to convince both of the thieves who were hanging on crosses on either side of Him. Only one was open to change. We can pray, we can cajole, we can challenge, but it is only God who can draw them with His goodness (Romans 2:4) and who grants them an opportunity to repent and change. Then they can be set free from their often self-inflicted torture through the knowledge of God's truth. It is only God's truth which can set people free (John 8:32). We are but simple tools in God's hands for such purposes.

Casting out demons is not for everyone. In Mark 6:7 and 6:13, we find that Jesus *"called unto him the twelve, and began to send them forth by two and two; and gave them power over unclean spirits; ...and they cast out many devils, and anointed with oil many that were sick, and healed them* [all]." But by the time we get to chapter 9 where the father brought his boy to the disciples for a cure, the disciples failed to cast out the deaf and dumb spirit. We also find out this boy has had the demon since he was a child.

The disciples asked Jesus what did they do wrong, and Jesus said their faith was not where it should be since it was smaller than a mustard seed. Jesus also stated that "this kind can come forth by nothing, but by prayer [and fasting]." So, it takes considerable more spiritual preparation to handle some tougher cases. Prior to the Lord's crucifixion, the apostles and disciples had no need to fast because the bridegroom (Christ) was still with them (Mark 2:20).

We also see that demons vary in power with some being more wicked than others. Matthew 12:45 states, "*Then [the demon] goes and takes along with it seven other spirits more wicked than itself, and they go in and live there; and the last state of that man becomes worse than the first.*" So, it stands to reason we need to be devoted to prayer and fasting.

Why fasting? When we sacrifice food and other fleshly desires to spend more time in God's word and in prayer to better equip ourselves for future trials, we can only grow in grace, knowledge, and faith – which is spiritual power.

Another interesting perspective is gleaned from Adam Clarke's commentary. In essence, he states that fasting on the part of the one being demonized goes a long way to kill the deeds of the flesh. He states, "that there are certain evil propensities, in some persons, which pampering the flesh tends to nourish and strengthen; and that self-denial and fasting, accompanied by prayer to God, are the most likely means, not only to mortify such propensities, but also to destroy them."

Consider someone addicted to alcohol. Fasting from alcohol and spending more time with God instead of at the bar will in all probability help rid that person of alcoholic behavior and reduce alcoholic-induced health issues. Prayer, coupled with repentance and obedience, is crucial to reprove, resist, and rebuke demonic activities. As the late Baptist preacher, Adrian Rodgers, once said, "When Satan knocks on a vibrant Christian's door, Jesus answers, and when Satan sees us obeying the Lord, he flees."

Today we deal with evil spirits not by finding someone who claims they have the ability to cast them out, but by following principles of Scripture. For example, 2Corinthians 2:10-11 states we should extend forgiveness, which is for our corporate and personal benefit, so that Satan doesn't take advantage of us, "for we are not ignorant of his schemes."

Ephesians 6:11-18 encourages us to *"put on the full armor of God"* so that we can stand firm against the schemes of the devil. This armor begins with knowing God's word (*"having girded your loins with truth"*). Then we are to avoid sin and obey God's word (*"put on the breastplate of righteousness"*).

These steps allow us to be prepared to share the Gospel and grow the kingdom and bring peace to troubled souls ("shod *your feet with the preparation of the gospel of peace"*). The *"shield of faith"* (verse 16) is our ability to rely on God to complete that which He has promised in His word (properly interpreted, of course), and not to rely on our feelings or experiences. The *"the helmet of salvation"* is our confidence of victory since nothing can remove us from the hands of God.

The *"sword of the Spirit,"* which is the word of God, is our only offensive piece of gear. With God's word, we can pull down strongholds or mental barriers, even assumptions and biases, people might have, since it is the means the Holy Spirit uses to convict the world of sin.

Ephesians 6:18 says we are to *"pray at all times in the Spirit, and with this in view, be on the alert with all perseverance and petition for all the saints."* Praying in the Spirit does not mean praying in tongues or with "vain repetitions." It means praying in God's will so we will get a positive answer to our prayers.

Praying in God's will begins with obedience to His word. To *"pray at all times in the Spirit"* does not mean to be on your knees 24x7, but to have a right relationship with God 24x7. To *"be on the alert"* means for us to be diligent with our praying, thoughtful, watchful, devoted to praying (Romans 12:12). God chooses to use our prayers as a means to accomplish His Kingdom work.

Other passages of Scripture that help us deal with evil spirits include James 4:7: *"Submit yourselves therefore to God. Resist the devil, and he will flee from you,"* and 1Peter 5:8-9, *"Be of sober spirit, be on the alert. Your adversary, the devil, prowls around like a roaring lion, seeking someone to devour. But resist him, firm in your faith, knowing that the same experiences of suffering are being accomplished by your brethren who are in the world."* Whenever anyone violates these principles of Scripture, whether believer or non-believer, they are at risk for demonic influence.

Convenient Christianity. Another aspect often overlooked in the lives of many who are financially, physically, mentally, relationally, or spiritually troubled is that of convenient Christianity. This is where we only obey God's commands when it is convenient for us to do so. For example, we seem to read our Bible when it is convenient. We pray, we give, and we keep the speed limit (the good laws of the land) when it is convenient for us. Another term for this convenient approach to life is taking the path of least resistance.

For the waywardness of the naive will kill them, and the complacency of fools will destroy them. Proverbs 1:32

We need to migrate from convenient Christianity to sincere Christianity. If we are serious about our relationship with the Lord, we will read our Bible, pray, keep the speed limit, and give whether it is convenient for us or not.

Remember once we start obeying the way God wants us to obey, God takes over responsibility for all of our needs. He becomes ultimately responsible for our total wellbeing. Whom would you prefer to have in control of your life – God or yourself? Our responsibility is to be obedient servants. God's responsibility is to mold us into the image of His Son.

The ultimate test of our faith is where does our faith reside? Is our faith in ourselves, in our bank accounts, in our circumstances, in our health, or in God? God truly wants to bless each of us more than we realize or can even comprehend. It may not be with the health and wealth we can envision for ourselves, but we need to be like the Apostle Paul and accept abundance or abject poverty, health or thorns in the flesh at God's hands.

Fortunately, God also gives us ample opportunities to improve our lot in life, though there might be limitations we need to learn to accept. There is nothing wrong with seeking health and wealth for ourselves and our loved ones, but Scripture is clear, there is no guarantee we will be given the blessings we want for ourselves. We have to come to terms that it is always better to accept the blessings God wants us to have and not be sent "leanness to our souls" (Psalms 106:15) because we preferred to chase after some fool's good.

Chapter 7
A Little More History on Pentecostalism

"If a [false] prophet or a dreamer of dreams arises among you and gives you a sign or a wonder, and the sign or the wonder comes true, … you shall not listen to the words of that prophet or that dreamer of dreams; for the LORD your God is testing you to find out if you love the LORD your God with all your heart and with all your soul.
Deuteronomy 13:1-4

My wife has three mentally handicapped brothers who have all participated in Special Olympics in their younger years. Their condition is related to something called Fragile-X syndrome, a genetic abnormality that affects neural development within a fetus, resulting in mental retardation. Each of these guys can run, jump, laugh, cry, get angry, give a hug, and fish (if you don't ask them to put on a worm). They can also eat, bathe, and shave without assistance, but they are not able to read, write or comprehend beyond the first grade level. Growing up with parents who attended Pentecostal churches, naturally they had numerous people praying for them, and even praying for their healing. Unfortunately, their IQ's never increased even by 1 point over the years. The parents often had to field such inquiries as to what sins had they possibly committed, and "you just need to have more faith."

The father's faith often slipped, partly as a result of him perceiving God was not being true to His word for not miraculously healing his boys. Over the years the parents prayed, confessed, and sought out other godly people for help and guidance, but all to no avail.

They were not alone. Numerous other Christians and non-Christians, alike, who suffer from similar debilitating organic disorders have never received healings either. Not since the time of Christ have any organic ailments been healed miraculously and instantaneously.

I even asked my father-in-law, before he passed away with cancer, why he would continue staying in a Pentecostal church even though it is quite provable their doctrine is poorly defined and more often than not, their experiences are not from God. His response was typical of Pentecostals. He basically said to me he knew the experiences he had, such as speaking in tongues, seeing a leg grow about two inches, and witnessing people cured of cancer, were real to him and he firmly believed his experiences were truly of God. His experience-based faith was unshaken even when I clearly showed him from Scripture that speaking gibberish is not biblical tongues, and God must be a cheap God if the best He can do is cure subjective functional ailments such as cancers and He can only grow a leg out by two inches, but has never restored one amputated limb or healed any organic ailments, such as mental retardation, since the time of Christ.

Hanging on to one's experiences as gospel truth is like a fish caught on a glimmering, tasty-looking hook. Even sound and logical reasoning will not always free someone who doesn't see themselves as hooked onto something false. Jesus saw this with the Pharisees and Sadducees He dealt with. The Pharisees and Sadducees were hooked on false teachings or "doctrines of men" of their own making.

The best we can do to convert a soul from the error of their ways is to continue to speak humbly and gently, argue wisely by giving a sound defense for the hope that lies within us, and let God be God. Perhaps, God will give them acknowledgement of the truth (2Timothy 2:25) as found in the Bible and not in their experiences.

The sad part about hanging onto misinterpreted doctrine and experiences is eventually, many will lose their faith and drop out of church as a result of God not performing as they expect Him to. The unfortunate legacy of the Pentecostal/Charismatic movement is not one of doctrinal purity or spiritual maturity but of doctrinal confusion and spiritual subjectivity. Pentecostals often error in doctrine because they inject a doctrine into a passage instead of extracting a doctrine from a passage, or they interpret "descriptive" passages such as what we often find in the Gospels and Acts as "prescriptive" for the Church age, and it just may not be so.

Why stay with a belief system if it fails to deliver on its promises? Faith runs deep in all of us. Often times the faith of our parents is good enough. Other times we latch onto a belief system if it met a dire need early in our life. After all, what Judeo-Christian faith does God fail to work with? Every Baptist, Methodist, Jew, Presbyterian, Pentecostal, Catholic, and a host of other denominations and fellowships within the Judeo-Christian camp lay claims to God answering prayers for them.

Everyone has a different reason for staying with or gravitating toward a particular type of church. Some Christians like the high tech entertainment aspects many churches have adopted. Others want a church that teaches and preaches sound doctrine rather than an experience-led approach. Still others prefer the hope of the miraculous to give them the sense that God is moving amongst them.

The rapid rise of the Pentecostal belief system along with its many and varied offshoots and waves deserves our attention. We need to figure out if it is truly a move of God whose bandwagon we should all jump on or possibly a move by Satan to prepare the naïve for the end times where "lying wonders" will be the norm.

PENTECOSTALISM'S POSITIVE EFFECTS ON CHRISTENDOM

Many Christians will agree that God has used Pentecostals and all their movements and offshoots to further the gospel message throughout the world. Pentecostal zeal to worship God and to share His truth and compassion within their church walls and without is not only admirable and commendable, but it is truly enviable and in some cases worth emulating.

Pentecostals may be faulted for their bizarre behavior, but all churches and denominations can be faulted for something. Many Baptists can be faulted for their stoicism, or lack of emotions and zeal in their worship. Catholics and Lutherans can be faulted for their liturgical or mechanical approach to worship. Again, God doesn't wait till we reach full maturity or perfect doctrine before He puts us to good use. He looks at our individual and collective hearts and molds us into a single unit with many diverse parts.

What is intriguing about God's sovereignty at times from our human perspective is His ability to even use the wicked to accomplish His will on earth. If God can corral the wicked and channel the heart of a king like water (Proverbs 21:1), He can easily shepherd each diverse church body to impact the lost. Even with the limited amount of Scripture and sound teachings that is presented in many Pentecostal-type churches, God can still use these churches to bring people to a saving knowledge of Him. Whether in pretense or in truth, Christ can still be proclaimed (Philippians 1:18).

Does this mean we should live and let live? Sometimes yes, and sometimes no. The disciples were ready to pounce on some others who were proclaiming Christ but doing it a different way. Jesus told them to let them be. If they are not against Him, then they are for Him (Mark 9:38-40).

We are commanded to look after one another's welfare, and there is a benefit to challenging each other's waywardness. The Apostle Paul says it this way, "*We proclaim Christ, admonishing everyone and teaching everyone with all wisdom, so that we may present everyone complete in Christ*" (Colossians 1:28). We should not be afraid to challenge others, as well as ourselves, in regards to sound doctrine – for by it, we save ourselves as well as others (1Timothy 4:16). Healings and miracles do not save. Only sound doctrine saves.

Brief History of Pentecostalism. Pentecostalism emerged almost exactly one hundred years ago. Precursors of Pentecostalism during the 19th century included Wesley's Methodism, the Keswick Convention in the UK, John Nelson Darby's 'dispensationalism', the divine healing movement, and John Alexander Dowie's utopian Zion City near Chicago. The Holiness (or 'Sanctification') movement that migrated from the UK to the United States in the early 1800's is considered by most historians to have had the most direct influence on Pentecostalism with its speaking in tongues and the working of various "ecclesiastical" signs and wonders.

Furthermore, Pentecostalism began as a racially integrated movement and included women in positions of leadership. Its beginnings were simultaneous with the organization of the Fundamentalist (or cessationist) movement, but distinct in many beliefs and practices. A series of revival meetings, called the Azusa Street Revival in Los Angeles, California, featured the "outpouring of the gifts of the Holy Spirit" is officially considered the beginnings of the Pentecostal movement. This revival started in April, 1906 and lasted until 1913. To their credit, thousands of Pentecostal missionaries went forth establishing missions throughout the world.

The First Wave. The early Pentecostals believed that the bestowal of these "latter rain" gifts of the Holy Spirit, such as speaking in tongues, were mission tools which would allow them to save the world for Christ before the end times. As it grew, the movement splintered into various cooperative fellowships, including Assemblies of God, Church of God in Christ, Church of God (Cleveland), and International Church of the Foursquare Gospel. Eventually, the movement would result in literally thousands of denominations worldwide. Today, the combined number of Pentecostals and related movements and waves is estimated at around 500 million people, or 25% of all Christians.

Many historians point to the Pentecostal movement starting with the preacher Charles F. Parham's Bethel Gospel School in Topeka, Kansas, where his student, Agnes Ozman, first spoke in tongues on January 1, 1900 or 1901 (historical records differ). Parham was an ex-Methodist, an independent preacher, and a healer in Kansas.

Agnes Ozman spoke in a tongue which sounded like "Chinese," though never actually verified. She is renowned as being the first Pentecostal person to ever speak in tongues. The problem with her tongue speaking is that it is claimed that she spoke nonstop for three days in Chinese, actually unable to speak in English until she was "released" to do so. Other students of Parham were alleged to have spoken in a variety of languages including Japanese, Hungarian, Syrian, Hindi, and Spanish.

Parham noted that "cloven tongues of fire" appeared over the heads of the speakers. Sometimes interpretations followed such as "God is love," "Jesus is mighty to save," and "Jesus is ready to hear." Parham also anticipated that missionaries could be sent out all over the world who would supernaturally speak in the native tongue of the land, without having studied it. It never happened, however, and Parham was extremely disappointed that his missionary plans were thwarted.[52]

Other eyewitnesses of the Azusa Street Revival reported seeing a holy glow emanating from the building that could be seen from streets away. Others reported hearing sounds from the wooden building like explosions that reverberated around the neighborhood. Such phenomena caused onlookers to call the fire department out on several occasions when a blaze or explosion was reported at the mission building. The Child Welfare Agency tried to shut down the meetings because

---

[52]http://settingcaptivesfree.me/tag/azusa-street-revival/.

there were unsupervised children within and around the building at all hours of the day and night. The Health Department tried to stop the meetings because they said the cramped quarters were unsanitary and a danger to public health. God-hungry Christians flocked in from everywhere.[53]

Though the Holiness movement with its tongues speaking and the working of prophecies, signs, and wonders was a precursor to Pentecostalism, it never grabbed the attention of the mainline denominations. From those humble beginnings in Los Angeles, however, Pentecostalism exploded onto the world scene, and has been labeled as the first wave.

Second and Third Waves. In the 1960s charismatic fever infiltrated many mainline denominations, becoming known as the Second Wave, and the Pentecostal tidal wave rolled on. In the 1980s more bizarre happenings came to the forefront and this became known as the Third Wave. Since the 1980s, the movement has overrun many Assemblies of God churches, as well as other Pentecostal churches, and has made incredible inroads into the larger body of Evangelicalism with its prosperity gospel and "Name-it-and-Claim-it" theology. It is not the Holy Spirit drawing converts into the movement by convicting their souls of the truth of the Gospel, but it is the allurement of prosperity and health.

In short, Pentecostalism grew from a fringe group to a conglomerate of denominations and independent churches with adherents around the world who are able to watch the latest teachings and happenings via television and the

---

[53]http://www.revival-library.org/pensketches/am_pentecostals/seymourazusa.html.

Internet. According to many Pentecostals, bizarre behavior does not always equate to false teachings. After all, didn't Isaiah walk around naked to proclaim his message, and didn't Jesus work the spectacular to win the lost?

Pentecostals, like many other Christians, claim there have been numerous movements of the Holy Spirit throughout church history from The Great Reformation, the First and the Second Great Awakenings, the Pietism and Holiness Movement, the Student Volunteer Movement, the Pentecostal Outpouring, the Latter Rain and Healing and Deliverance Movements, all within the loosely defined first, second, third, and a recently acknowledged fourth wave movements.

Other expressions of Pentecostalism include the Jesus People, Word of Faith or Name-it-and-Claim-it adherents, the Prophetic Movement and the New Apostolic Reformation. Within each of these movements or waves there have been the contributing revival peaks such as with the Korean Church Growth, the Argentine Outpouring, the Chinese Underground Church Movement, the Cell Church explosion with its many expressions, the Toronto Blessing, the Brownsville Revival, and many others.

Pentecostals also claim that every wave of the Holy Spirit has restored truths to the larger body of Christ and often even birthed entire new denominations and or ministries. After all, the nature of the Holy Spirit, as seen in Genesis 1:2 ("*The Spirit of God moved upon the face of the waters*"), is to move and to keep moving.

THE DANGERS OF BELIEVING IN PENTECOSTALISM

The problem with Pentecostalism is that biblical truth has never been restored by any of their movements. Challenged, maybe, but never restored. Instead, Pentecostalism has distorted, manipulated, abrogated, and even ignored God's truth as they elevate experientialism over the clear teachings of the Bible.

The uniqueness of the apostolic era, along with the lack of any explicit teaching on the cessation of the supernatural gifts, might suggest we should be open to their continuance. But a lack of explicit teaching on a subject does not mean Scripture is vague about a particular subject. The concept of the Trinity is a prime example – it is an established truth within most of Christendom, but we lack any explicit passages on the topic. Also, the arguments for the closing of the Canon and the ceasing of inspired, infallible revelation impose that modern prophecies, tongues, knowledge, and wisdom stand or fall together.

Pentecostals do have some good arguments which we need to consider. For example, if signs, wonders, and power of the Holy Spirit were essential in bearing witness to the gospel in the first century, then why not now? Also, since through Christ our relationship with God has been restored, then there must be a restoration of benefits. To be free from sin is to be free from the curse of sin, which includes sickness, handicaps, and even death. It is narrow-minded, according to Pentecostals, to believe that Christ has conquered death but not disease.

Pentecostals do acknowledge that *"it is appointed unto man once to die and after this the judgment"* (Hebrews 9:27). God did not promise we would live forever in our current earthly bodies, but what Jesus did was to remove the sting of death. Our process of dying should therefore, according to Pentecostals, not be accompanied with pain and suffering. This "divine health" should be the norm for believers. Believers should leave this world like Moses and Caleb did, who were vigorous well into their twilight years. Moses was 120 years old when he died, and *"his eye was not dim, nor his vigor abated"* (Deuteronomy 34:7); and it is stated of Caleb in Joshua 14:11 when he was 85-years-old, *"I am still as strong today as I was in the day Moses sent me; as my strength was then, so my strength is now, for war and for going out and coming in."*

Should Moses' and Caleb's vitality and longevity be the norm or the exception for believers today? Consider King David, a prophet and a man after God's own heart, who had to snuggle up to a young lady, Abishag, to keep warm in his old age (1Kings 1:1-4). He died being about 70 years old. Another godly man, Barzillai, who sustained King David during his flight from Saul said, "*I am now eighty years old. Can I distinguish between good and bad? Or can your servant taste what I eat or what I drink? Or can I hear anymore the voice of singing men and women?"* Both these godly men were in waning heath and died before attaining the age of Moses and Caleb.

Solomon, the wisest man on earth (though not very prudent) relates in Ecclesiastes 12:1-6 the typical infirmities of growing old, to include bad eye sight and hearing, weak posture, feebleness, and lack of appetite. So, when we consider the whole counsel of God we acquire a different perspective than what Pentecostals hold to – divine health is not what they make it out to be. For Pentecostals to cite Moses and Caleb as prime examples for divine healing is bad hermeneutics. They fail to consider the whole counsel of God.

Faith healers themselves and even their immediate family members suffered and often died from various ailments, thereby annulling their teachings on divine healings. Kathryn Kulman (1907-1976) had heart problems, and died soon after having open heart surgery at 68 years of age. Kuhlman traveled extensively around the United States and in many other countries holding "healing crusades" between the 1940s and 1970s. Following a 1967 fellowship in Philadelphia, Dr. William A. Nolen conducted a case study of 23 people who claimed to have been cured during her services. Nolen's long-term follow-ups concluded that there were no cures in those cases. One woman who was said to have been cured of spinal cancer threw away her brace and ran across the stage at Kuhlman's command; her spine collapsed the next day, according to Nolen, and she died four months later.[54]

Faith healer Smith Wigglesworth (1859-1947), though he lived a long life of 88 years, suffered for years with kidney stones.[55] John G. Lake (187-1935) suffered and died from a stroke at 65 years of age.[56] Aimee Semple McPherson (1890-1944) died at 53 most likely from an accidental overdose compounded by kidney failure.[57] Kenneth Hagin's sister and a

---

[54]http://en.wikipedia.org/wiki/Kathryn_Kuhlman.

[55]http://en.wikipedia.org/wiki/Smith_Wigglesworth.

[56]http://en.wikipedia.org/wiki/John_G._Lake.

[57]http://en.wikipedia.org/wiki/Aimee_Semple_McPherson.

son-in-law died of cancer. Hagin was considered the "Father" of the Word of Faith Movement. No faith healer or their family members are immune from sickness and disease.

Another case in point is John Wimber. Wimber is probably the most prominent modern contemporary Third Wave healer, but he died of a brain hemorrhage on November 17, 1997, aged 63, following a fall and recent coronary bypass surgery.

When faith healers get sick where do they go? To another faith healer, or to the next tent meeting or miracle crusade? NO! They do what most of us do and go to their physicians for medication, surgery, and therapy. Pentecostals have to acknowledge the sting of death is real, and claiming to possess the gifts and the faith to avoid that sting is not obvious even to the most ardent Pentecostal.

Another good argument Pentecostals have is that Satan comes to steal and destroy (John 10:10), and some of his greatest weapons are sickness and disease, which steals our joy, time, and productivity away from accomplishing the Lord's work. What Pentecostals fail to grasp is that even sickness and disease can also accomplish God's will for our lives and for His kingdom. Psalms 119:71 states that "*It is good for me that I was afflicted, That I may learn Your statutes.*" Plus, the teachings gleaned from the book of Job yield rich dogma on how even satanic catastrophes, illnesses, and death fit in with molding us into the image of Christ.

I am not trying to twist my way out of the teachings of Scripture on healings. I am trying to convey the whole counsel of God on this matter. If we are unbalanced and only teach one side or the other, we are going to miss teaching sound doctrine. On one side, we could fall into the "name-it-and-claim-it" bleachers which affords only psychosomatic healings at best, and on the other side we could miss the true and biblical escape from sickness and death by shortchanging ourselves on what Scripture prescribes for acquiring and maintaining our mental, physical, emotional, physiological, and spiritual health.

Luke tells us of a woman who was afflicted physically by a "*spirit*" for 18 long years (Luke 13:10-17) –"*she was bent double, and could not straighten up at all*" (verse 11). Jesus "*freed*" her from her sickness, and attributed her illness to the work of Satan. Are there people today, much like this woman described in Luke 13, with illnesses directly caused by Satan and his horde of demons? There is no scriptural evidence to deny such works of Satan today.

For Pentecostals to harp on this particular type of Satanic or demonic activity is actually a good thing for the church at large to be sensitive to, and realize the need to free people from such a demonic hold. The process is not a laborious exercise with magical incantations as Pentecostals make it out to be. Demonic release should be just as simple as Jesus makes it out to be – instantaneous and complete. Resist the devil and he will flee.

"But wait a minute," you might ask, "Isn't demonic release a supernatural event?" Since we are dealing with entities outside of our physical space, time, and material dimensions (i.e., demons), yes, it is a supernatural event, but we are not breaking any natural or physical laws to release demons from their hold on individuals. Remember we are not wrestling against flesh and blood but against the spiritual rulers, powers, forces of wickedness in the heavenly places (Ephesians 6:12).

Are modern-day faith healers and miracle workers frauds? There are undoubtedly wolves scamming the flock since false teachings abound, but we can give many of faith-healing advocates the benefit of the doubt and say they are well-meaning in their intentions of truly trying to heal people in the name of Christ, but they at least are self-deceived. Their healings are not of God, but of psychosomatic means at best and demonic means at worst. Their prophecies and tongues are either from self or from demonic forces, but they are not of God.

More Historical Evidence for the Miraculous. Historical claims by the Didache (a brief early Christian treatise, dated by most scholars to the late first or early 2nd century) spoke of prophets continuing into the second century; and even the Reformers gave serious treatment to the matter of signs, wonders and prophetic claims. Martin Luther (1483-1546) believed the power to do signs was available in his day, and John Calvin (1509-1564) allowed for extraordinary gifts "as the need of the times demands."[58] Therefore, as Pentecostals claim, the fact that miracles do appear throughout history, even sporadically, proves miracles have never ceased – at least ecclesiastical type miracles which are inferior to those recorded by Jesus and His apostles.

---

[58]John F. MacArthur, J. (1992). *Charismatic Chaos.* Grand Rapids: Zondervan Publishing House. 166-168.

Subjective Manifestations. God is a God who hides Himself from those who don't want to find Him (Isaiah 45:15), yet He is also a God who reveals Himself to those who come looking or *"draw near"* to Him (James 4:8). Those who examine the evidence will see God's fingerprints everywhere. Others won't believe even if someone were to honestly rise from the dead (Luke 16:31).

Naturally, Pentecostals believe God is manifesting Himself to them at an unprecedented rate, and this is evident with all the purported healings, miracles, and dreams. Yet, every one of their healings, miracles, and dreams are very subjective even after Pentecostal teachings have been gaining ground for more than 100 years. Where are the miracles of Jesus, of Peter, and of Paul – the *"noteworthy miracles that are apparent to all"* and *"cannot be denied"* (Acts 4:16)? We can only conclude they ceased with the Apostolic era of the first century.

Answered Prayers Are Subjective. God doesn't want to force anyone to believe in Him, so God provides ample wiggle room for skeptics to disbelieve, yet be held fully accountable for all eternity for their decisions. Answered prayers, though subjective, are however, the best response we have to address the concerns of skeptics.

Evolutionists believe everything happens by chance with no intelligent forethought. Unfortunately, evolutionary dogma has even crept into the church and undermined the Gospel by weakening the plain teachings of Scripture as found in the first 11 chapters of Genesis – which are the foundation of the rest of the Bible, including the Gospel message. If the first Adam was a mythical creature, the second Adam had no reason to die. If we can't trust the Bible when we are told in historical prose that men lived over 900 years and vegetation was around before the sun was created, then why believe that someone had to die for our sins? Even the Assemblies of God, a Pentecostal denomination, recently adopted a revised statement on "The Doctrine of Creation" that opens the door to evolution and millions of years, and the various compromise positions on Genesis held by some in the church (such as gap theory, day age, progressive creation, and theistic evolution).[59] As seen by this, Pentecostals continue to slip down that slippery slope of biblical non-relevance and trivializing once fundamentally-held teachings of Scripture.

Pentecostals can be credited for bringing enthusiasm back into many churches, but they can also be credited with bringing heresy into the churches. They can be credited for breaking down racial barriers within the church walls, but they can also be accused of bringing liberal theology into its ranks. Often times signs and wonders are elevated over truth within Pentecostal circles. Pentecostals, Charismatics, and 3rd Wavers are unable to defend their positions that the Canon is closed since they believe prophetic utterances and new revelations are still possible from God. Pentecostals admittedly find themselves very open to any and all expressions of miraculous works, including demonic. And believers are often categorized according to their giftedness instead of fruitfulness, and they have an inherent danger of elitism on one side and inferiority on the other.

---

[59]http://blogs.answersingenesis.org/blogs/ken-ham/2010/09/08/a-sad-day-for-the-assemblies-of-god-denomination/

CHAPTER 8
CONCLUSION

⁂

In the same way the Spirit also helps our weakness; for we do not know how to pray as we should, but the Spirit Himself intercedes for us with groanings too deep for words. Romans 8:26

⁂

As much as we would love to see every Christian come to the same doctrinal stance that God would have us to reach, we must realize getting everyone on the same page is not possible in a fallen world. Basically, we all believe what we want to believe, and the vast majority of people do not leave the religious system they grew up in. For the most part, Catholics stay Catholics, Baptists stay Baptists, Pentecostals stay Pentecostals, Mormons stay Mormons, Muslims stay Muslims, and Jews stay Jews – with only a small percentage ever migrating away from the faith of their parents.

That is a study in itself why we are so convinced the faith of our parents is almost unquestionable. A part of that study would include the gullibility of people. The younger a person is the more gullible and naïve they tend to be – sometimes that is good, other times, not so good. After all, look at your typical jihadist terrorist whose average age is in the early 20's. A Catholic priest once told me, "Give us a child till their 12 years old, and we have them for life." On the good side, most evangelical churches, such as Baptists, often tout that the majority of believers accept Christ while in their pre-teen years.

It is imperative for all rational and reasonable people to evaluate their beliefs at some point during their lifetime (whether they be Christian, non-Christian, agnostic, or even atheistic), and adjust as needed to be more in line with sound doctrine.

As we saw in Chapter 2, Jesus healed anybody and everybody of anything and everything, anytime and every time, anywhere and everywhere He went with a simple touch or with just a few words. No lengthy, agonizing prayers were ever uttered by the Lord or even by His apostles. All healings were quick, instantaneous, complete, painless, and permanent, and are nothing like the purported miracles of today.

Since Pentecostals claim that Jesus is the same yesterday, today, and forever; and that what transpired in the Gospels and in the book of Acts should be every bit evident in our day and age, then we need to ask the hard questions. Why can't or doesn't God heal the hard cases (i.e., the organic cases)? Why does He heal only the easy cases, the psychosomatic or functional cases? Why are the so-called miracles we see in Pentecostal churches of the same types and caliber we see witch doctors, Hindus, Buddhists, Catholics, hypnotists, and even Satanists perform? And why do Pentecostal churches have the same ratio of people with cancer, near-sightedness, far-sightedness, hypertension, autism, obsessive compulsive disorders (OCD), attention deficit disorders (ADD), and death as in other churches?

We can only come to several conclusions. Either we have contradictions in the Bible, or we have misinterpreted the Bible. Since God's word is incontrovertible, we have to acknowledge that God is no longer working supernatural miracles. That means He has opted to only work providentially until such time we enter into the chaotic period of the Great Tribulation and God brings two very special witnesses onto the world scene.

Even Jesus could not convince but a few hundred Jews out of thousands who listened to Him and who witnessed firsthand His signs and wonders. Some saw Jesus as a threat who needed to die. Others saw Him as a miracle-vending machine. Only a few came to realize the truth of His deity and His mission. Many of those early disciples died a martyr's death trying to convince others of the benefits to changing their old false doctrines for sound teachings which would lead them to eternal life in Heaven and an abundant life while here on earth – not an abundance of things, but an abundance of meaning and purpose.

Though Jesus might have worked over 100,000 healings and miracles during His three-year ministry, they still were not enough to convince everyone or even to satisfy the most critical opponent. After many of His disciples left Him, Jesus asked His closest disciples, *"will you leave Me too?"* Peter's response was *"where would we go? You have the words of life."*

Even if the only work God performed for us was to give us His holy word, shouldn't that be enough? After all, what does God owe to any of us? May our faith be as strong as Job's where we can say *"shall we not receive evil from the hand of the Lord as well as good?...though He should slay me, yet will I trust him"* (Job 2:10; 13:15).

One recent success story of a church denomination forsaking some heretical doctrines involved the Worldwide Church of God (WCG), founded by Herbert W. Armstrong in the 1930s. Throughout the 1990s, Hank Hanegraaff, president of Christian Research Institute (CRI), renowned for being the radio voice of *The Bible Answer Man,* engaged in dialogue with leaders of the WCG. The WCG had long been regarded as a cult by evangelicals, primarily for its denial of the Trinity. Following Armstrong's death in 1986, WCG re-evaluated many of its own teachings, including the British-Israel doctrine and erroneous eschatological predictions. Hanegraaff, a staunch critic of the Word of Faith movement yet a staunch proponent of classical Pentecostalism, was one of a handful of evangelical apologists who assisted in their reforms.

WCG, now known as Grace Communion International (GCI), is accepted among evangelicals since they adopted the doctrine of the Trinity and salvation by grace through faith. This example shows not only is it possible for individuals to migrate from false teachings, but even entire denominations. All that is needed is an honest evaluation of Scripture along with any and all held assumptions and biases.

If cessationism is indeed correct, and God is not in the business today of even healing a paper cut miraculously, then we should expect such truth would impact our everyday life. Our prayer life, our teaching and discipleship approaches, and even our witnessing approaches are affected by our core doctrines.

For example, in our prayer life, though a cessationist may pray for God's direct intervention and quick healing for a loved one, we realize *"all things will work out for our good"* and for His glory. This means God will work through the body's own healing process along with maneuvering situations such as finding the right medication, the right treatment, the timely and correct prognoses, and any rehabilitation to expedite a cure.

Now, there is nothing wrong in asking God for an instantaneous cure since we are commanded to pray for any and all things and for any and all men. God takes our weak and maybe even erroneous prayers, as Romans 8:25 says, *"the Spirit Himself intercedes for us with groanings too deep for words"* into a meaningful and answerable prayer.

SUBJECTIVITY OF PRAYERS

God chooses to use our prayers to accomplish His will in Heaven and on earth, to change the course of man's history, and to boldly proclaim the truth of the Gospel. God's sovereign will for mankind will be accomplished down to the micro-second whether we pray or not. We are commanded throughout Scripture to know God's will for our lives, to pray unceasingly, pray fervently and persistently, be devoted to prayer, and to pray and watch with expectation for positive answers.

Since God is no longer healing or working miracles instantaneously, from a cessationist's viewpoint, then it stands to reason our prayers will not always get answered instantaneously. If we pray for a job, a spouse, good health, or sundry other things it could take some time before God brings a complete answer through providence.

Yet, it is such prayers that become the best answer we have for skeptics, though the answers to our prayers may appear subjective, coincidental, and speculative. Remember God is not out to force anyone to believe, but He gives ample evidence to make a sound decision. God knows everyone's needs even before we ask Him (Matthew 6:8).

Even the prayers of the apostles and disciples in the Epistles reflect subjective outcomes. Paul prayed that the love amongst the Philippians would *"abound still more and more in real knowledge and all discernment"* (Philippians 1:9). This would not be answered instantaneously, but over time as they experienced obstacles, challenges, belligerent people, unruly rulers, and other worldly challenges and church entanglements. Paul also prayed for the Ephesians to be enlightened so they would know what is the hope of the Lord's calling and what are the riches of the glory of His inheritance in the saints (Ephesians 1:18).

John prayed that his audience would *"prosper and be in good health"* (3John 1:2). Again, this would involve the element of time along with good and bad experiences. They would not be expected to receive instant cash or the instant removal of belly fat without some hard work and discipline. Sure, a rich relative could suddenly die and leave an inheritance unexpectedly, but even that is a providential happenstance. The writer of Hebrews asked his audience to pray for him and his entourage of other disciples that they would conduct themselves honorably in all things (Hebrews 13:8). There is no hint of instantaneous spontaneity with these prayers.

When Jesus prayed for His apostles and for all future believers in John 17 He asked the Father to *"keep them in Your name"* (v11), *"keep them from the evil one"* (v15), *"sanctify them in the truth"* (v17), *"make them one"* (v21), and eventually *"let them see My glory"* (v25). This grandiose prayer by the Lord is one that is still being answered today in the life of every

Christian. Though there might be disunity among many within the church, yet, we will one day see this prayer fully answered as we stand before Jesus in all of His glory, fully united in worship and adoration in the spirit and in truth.

Even the Lord's Prayer, in Luke 11, reflects an element of time. In that model prayer we have the privilege to ask for daily bread, but that bread would not be materializing out of thin air as it did when Jesus fed the crowds of 5,000 and 4,000 men, but from providence, and providence involves the element of time.

Some would protest this most vehemently, and be able to recount stories of hearing of parents and grandparents and missionaries telling of lean meals able to feed many. Consider this, however – if nothing is too hard for God and he performed a supernatural miracle of multiplying a meal, then why hasn't God restored a single missing leg? Better yet, why hasn't God given the hungry a full belly of nutritious food without even having to eat something? We need to honestly think through the so-called supernatural wonders we hear from time to time and assess them from what is clearly taught in Scripture.

Subjective answers to our prayers offer the skeptics with enough evidence to see the hand of the God who "hides Himself" working providentially on behalf of His saints. Yet, they have enough wiggle room not to believe and still be fully accountable for their decision. When atheists, agnostics, and skeptics stand before God on that fearful day of judgment they will only have themselves to blame for ending up in Hell.

There are over 300 incidences in the Bible referencing praying. The very first mention of a prayer being uttered with a positive answer is found in Genesis 20:17. Abraham prayed to God on behalf of Abimelech, and God healed Abimelech and his wife and maids so they could once again have children after Abimelech released Sarah from his harem unharmed. Why God would seemingly condone a form of polygamy by answering a prayer for an adulterer and an idolater is beyond us all. In other passages where Israel was in a state of adultery and idolatry God told Jeremiah more than once not to pray for such sinners (Jeremiah 7:16; 11:14; 14:11). God's people are always held to a higher standard.

In the places in Scripture where God instantaneously and supernaturally answered prayers it was always within the timeframe of when He was working amongst His prophets, priests, and judges (Moses, Elijah, Elisha, Daniel, Isaiah, Gideon, Samson, etc.), His Son, and His apostles. For example, Elijah in 1Kings 17:21 called to the Lord, "*O Lord, my God, I pray, let this child's life return to him*" and God restored to life the son of a widow who fed Elijah on one of his travels through her township.

Elijah is also mentioned in James 5:17-18 in a very unique way. James says, "*Elijah was a man with a nature like ours, and he prayed earnestly that it would not rain, and it did not rain on the earth for three years and six months. Then he prayed again, and the sky poured rain and the earth produced its fruit.*" This passage has some nice considerations for us. James leads into this passage by highlighting in verse 16 that the fervent prayers of a righteous man accomplish much. Can we pray for rain and sunshine and other big things as Elijah prayed for? Absolutely! That is the point James is making.

Now when rain or sunshine comes forth as a result of our prayers, there is an element of subjectivity with it as we discussed previously. God brings the rain or sunshine as He sees fit to answer, and the element of time is involved. There are no natural laws being broken, so skeptics can still claim coincidence.

Please notice that James did not highlight Elijah's prayer for God to restore life to the widow's dead son, which would indicate we too should be able to pray for such supernatural and instantaneous wonders. Instead, James encourages us to pray for big things for God to work providentially not only in our lives but also nationally. After all, Elijah's prayer for rain and drought was to affect the entire region he lived in. In like fashion, we too can lift up prayers for God to bring blessings or testings, on a national scale or even a global scale. So let us pray big things for God's glory.

Can we pray for things too big for God to answer? The answer to that question depends on whether or not the prayer was within or outside of God's will. For example, if we petition the Lord to meet our need for food and clothing, it is quite feasible for God to come through, assuming we have not been frivolous with the resources He has given us already. On the other hand, if we were to ask God to put a trillion bucks into our bank account this time tomorrow, most would see the lunacy of that request. Pentecostals, however, claim nothing is too big for God, and there is no harm in asking for such big things, just in case He would provide. Such a flamboyant request falls into the "asking amiss" category where it would be consumed upon one's own lusts (James 4:3).

Be aware of this, Satan has no problems answering our frivolous requests which are outside of the will of God. That is part of his deceptive schemes often missed by Christians. Christians are duped into thinking they got an answer from God, when in effect they received a "lying wonder" and a leanness to their soul, whether it was for a physical healing or a financial solution.

We think if we were to ask God for bread, a loving and compassionate God wouldn't give us a stone; or if we were to ask Him for a fish sandwich, we wouldn't receive a snake in its stead (Luke 11:11). It is bad enough we reduce God to a magician or a miracle-vending machine when we ask Him to find us a close parking space at the store, or to help us find our car keys, or to help our Bundt cake turn out. True, God is concerned about all the small details in our lives, and this is where God's angels are possibly deployed as "*ministering spirits for them who shall be heirs of salvation*" (Hebrews 1:14).

We have to watch out for coming to God for help when we can do something for ourselves. That is called slothfulness. Recall what happened in John 6:24-27 where those who were fed among the crowd of 5,000 men did not receive their second request for a free meal. Some chased after Jesus as He crossed the Sea of Galilea looking for another free meal, only to be rebuked by him for laboring after the meat that perishes instead of seeking after the food which endures to eternal life. Their perspective was wrong. They had an earthly perspective and not a heavenly one, so they did not receive what they had asked for, though they had asked for their daily bread.

Providential Answers. Where we lack wisdom to figure out how to improve one's physical, mental, social, and financial wellbeing, we have the command to ask for such wisdom (James 1:5), and God will provide such wisdom liberally. Even if we were to run into demonic activity, we have God's guidance to combat such evil using His word as highlighted in Ephesians 6, where we are commanded to obey God's word for things to go well for everyone.

Like the Israelite's of old, once they crossed into the Promised Land, God stopped the supernatural miracles of daily manna, the visible presence of His guiding Angel, the visible leading through smoke and fire, and clothes and shoes not wearing out – and started to work providentially behind the scenes to destroy their enemies and advance His kingdom – assuming they obeyed His commands.

If continuationists (Pentecostals, Charismatics, and 3rd Wavers) are correct and supernatural healings, miracles, and other wonders and miraculous gifts of the Holy Spirit are still continuing today, then why don't we see confirmed cases of organic disorders being healed such as missing limbs restored, Down Syndrome kids healed, burn victims healed, broken bones immediately healed, soldiers on the battled field instantly healed of devastating injuries, and even paper cuts healed instantaneously as Jesus and His apostles and early disciples did it?

Albeit, any and all supernatural miracles claimed today by continuationists are admittedly of lesser quality and quantity of what was worked during the first century. We should at least see more than functional disorders being healed.

Again, is anything too hard for God? The obvious answer is NO; nothing is too hard for an omnipotent and omniscient God who is sovereign over His creation! Isn't it just as easy for God to restore an amputee's missing limb or to heal a Down Syndrome child as it is to heal someone with a headache? Absolutely. Therefore, if God is not healing the hard cases such as amputations and mental retardations, which are no harder for God to heal than a headache, what makes us think God is instantaneously healing the headaches, and cancers, and backaches, and other subjective healings we keep hearing about? He is not.

Could it be it is because it is not God's will to work supernatural miracles these days? Also, consider how many continuationists have to wear reading glasses, take prescription medicine, and how many die without being resurrected. It is the same ratio as in all other types of cessationist churches.

ETERNAL BLESSINGS AWAIT THE HANDICAPPED

God says He is the one who makes the lame and the blind (Exodus 4:11). Therefore, the handicapped need not fret about being short-changed in this life. Better days are coming for them. Isaiah 42:16 says the blind will be blessed with sight and not forsaken when the Lord comes. In other words, the handicapped will be made whole.

Another passage in Isaiah says, "*For this is what the LORD says: 'To the eunuchs* (i.e., the handicapped) *who keep my Sabbaths, who choose what pleases me and hold fast to my covenant— to them I will give within my temple and its walls a memorial and a name better than sons and daughters; I will give them an everlasting name that will not be cut off"* (Isaiah 56:4-5). This passage reveals the handicapped who remain faithful to God will receive higher esteem throughout Eternity than the non-handicapped!

We are also told in Micah 4:6-7 that God will assemble the lame (i.e., the handicapped) and outcasts, those whom He has afflicted, into a strong nation; and Zephaniah 3:19 says God will greatly honor the lame and outcasts in all the earth.

It should be abundantly clear from Scripture that the handicapped will eventually be eternally blessed for enduring the hardships God uniquely bestowed upon them during their relatively short lifetime. If you think about it, we all have endured or will endure some kind of handicap while traversing this life. Whether it is the feebleness acquired just from growing old, or a physical defect from birth – God determined it. In effect, we all will be blessed and rewarded, some more than others. Not only will we reap rewards for living righteously and faithfully expounding the Gospel, but also on the degree of hardships God has given each of us to endure.

The real power of God is not in receiving temporary healings and short-lived miracles as much as it is to permanently change lives for all eternity, where unbelievers become believers, and believers become conformed to the image of Christ.

Jesus said, "*…do not work for the food which perishes, but for the food which endures to eternal life*" (John 6:27). So let's stop chasing after temporal stuff and focus on the eternal. God's power (dynamite) to change lives is available to anyone willing to abide in Him (John 15).

Here is the final test. If a friend says to you, "Hey, did you hear at the new church down the street while they were preaching the gospel and speaking in tongues that some blind folks received their sight, others in wheelchairs got up and walked, even someone with cancer got cured, others threw their hearing aids away, an arm grew back, and a dead person was raised up? Come and see!"

How do you respond? Try these simple questions:

- Was everyone healed that sought for a healing, or only some?
- Can you confirm the organic healings (i.e., the arm growing back and the resurrection)?
- Is the faith healer overwhelmed with crowds looking for a healing, that wherever the faith-healer goes he cannot find time to eat; or does he wrap up his show within the hour and disappear with the offerings?
- Were the tongues spoken in known human languages, and were the interpretations accurate?

If your friend asks you why you are so skeptical, so unbelieving of the impossible happening at the hands of God, you can state: "God commands us to prove all things and not to chase after those false christs or false prophets who arise, and who can show signs and wonders such as miraculous healings to lead astray or confuse or impede the spiritual growth, if possible, of the very elect of God."

We have to admit that what we see today is a large number of people seeking healings, but few actually getting healed – and only of psychosomatic functional disorders. There have been no confirmed and substantiated resurrections or supernatural healings of organic disorders since the time of Christ and His Apostles.

Therefore, we have to conclude, based on Scriptural evidence as well as historical and observational data, that God has suspended working supernatural healings and miracles from the end of the Apostolic era till the two witnesses appear on the world scene, as depicted in Revelation 11. This includes the cessation of the gifts of the Holy Spirit. Revelatory prophecies, tongues, interpretation of tongues, knowledge, wisdom, healings and miracles are no longer being worked by God as depicted in Scripture. Pentecostals have, therefore, greatly fallen into the trap of Satan thinking God is still working supernatural miracles today. They neither understand the Scriptures nor the true power of God.

As I said in the preface of this book, I had a quandary about writing this book. Even if this book was to go viral and every Christian was to read it, I do not believe it would make a big difference to the majority of people, because people, for the most part, believe what they want to believe. People prefer to stay within their comfort zones. If people are drawn away beyond their comfort zone, it is usually in the chase for glitter and glamour. Few chase after the truth of God's word, which lacks the pizzazz Satan envelops around his entanglements.

As we can imagine for the last days Satan is setting the stage when he will deceive many believers and non-believers alike by the means of the miraculous. He is using false healings, false tongues, false miracles and other lying wonders as a warm up for his finale when he plans to deceive the vast majority of the world. If he can deceive God's people with the spectacular, then others will fall like dominos when his time has reached its zenith.

If we would honestly evaluate our experiences in light of God's word, we would see we have something better that works for both established churches in Christianized lands and for new upstart churches in heathen lands. This is the whole counsel of God, His completed revelation, the Bible – which is the only thing able to bring total, permanent, and complete healings for the soul.

It is only God's truth found in His word which converts a Hell-bound sinner into a Heaven-bound saint and transforms an immature believer into a mature emissary of God. We should live by faith and love, not by sight and sound. May God receive the glory due His name for all of His wondrous works He has done in the past and for what He will do.

I will remember the works of the LORD: surely I will remember thy wonders of old. Psalms 77:11

MORE ABOUT THE AUTHOR

Rod was raised in a Catholic family, but accepted Christ in a Pentecostal church where he met his future wife, Karen. Over several years and through continued study in God's word, they saw flagrant discrepancies between the Bible and the historical and modern Pentecostal/Charismatic movements, which prompted them to leave their Pentecostal teachings and migrate away from experience-based churches and toward more bible-centric churches having non-Pentecostal leanings. After living in the Washington, D.C. area for over 20 years, plus several years in England, and recently moving back to his home state of Kentucky he has witnessed, like everyone else, the far reaching influence of Pentecostalism. Pentecostal fervor and zeal is enviable, but it is overshadowed by blatant false teachings and practices, which should be continuously challenged.

Other books by Rod O'Neil include the following:

Guide to Benevolence Giving for Church and Family, 2009, Holy Fire Publishing, ISBN: 978-1-60383-203-8.

Scripture Index

Scripture Index

SCRIPTURE INDEX

Scripture Index

Scripture Index

CPSIA information can be obtained at www.ICGtesting.com
Printed in the USA
LVOW06s0432110414

381152LV00004B/395/P

9 781603 834865